Haunted or Not?

A step-by-step guide to investigating any house that seems haunted

Fiona Broome

New Forest Books

DISCLAIMER

Information in this book is based on personal experience and anecdotal evidence. It should not replace legal, medical, religious or other professional advice. Readers assume full responsibility for the use of the information in this book.

Every case is different, and we don't always know what spiritual entities we're dealing with. Do not follow *any* advice in this book if it makes you uncomfortable or uneasy.

If you are concerned about your safety, get help immediately, *in your community,* not online. Usually, it's best to speak with someone *trained and experienced* in spiritual matters, such as a priest or minister.

Before visiting any "haunted" site, verify the its location, accessibility, and safety.

No portion of this book may be reproduced in any form without written permission from the publisher or author, except as permitted by U.S. copyright law.

Contents

Important

If you feel that you are in danger from something in your home, do not stay there. Leave right now.

Then, get help from a professional *in real life,* not online.

Online predators and trolls can be far more dangerous than at least 99% of any ghostly activity in your home.

If you are uneasy about *anything* recommended in this book, don't try it. At this point, *everything* we think we know about ghosts is speculative. I'm simply reporting what's worked for me and my associates, over the past decades. My advice is anecdotal, and I cannot offer any guarantees regarding the results.

Ghosts are *spirits,* so a *spiritual* advisor – such as a trusted priest or other minister of your faith, in your town or community – may have the most experience with this kind of problem.

If they cannot help, ask them for a *trusted* referral or *personal* recommendation. Do not ask for help from strangers, online.

Introduction

For over 30 years, I've investigated houses that seem haunted.

Here's what I've learned: Most of them aren't *actually* haunted. (But those that are... wow!)

In this book, I'll explain how to tell the difference.

Oh, I have no doubt that spiritual entities – sometimes people from our past – visit or even linger in our world.

But first, if you feel at risk in your home, stay somewhere else until answers are found.

The next step is: Rule out normal explanations. For that, we'll turn to science. Real science.

In the words of Sherlock Holmes, "When you have eliminated all which is impossible, then whatever remains, however improbable, must be the truth." ~ Arthur Conan Doyle, in *The Case-Book of Sherlock Holmes*

That's how I investigate haunted sites: I use science to eliminate everything that might just *seem* ghostly.

So, if you think your home might be haunted – or you're an aspiring ghost hunter – this book is for you.

First, a few important notes...

Two important things to know about haunted houses

First, from my research, about 80% of homes that *seem* haunted aren't actually haunted.

In this book, you'll learn how to tell the difference.

Second, even if your home *has* a ghost, it's probably not like what you've seen on TV and in movies.

Few ghosts are evil. Even fewer can cause physical harm.

What you'll learn

First, I'm going to explain what might be dangerous – or even life-threatening – in any home or other location that *seems* haunted.

Then, I'll help you "debunk" your home. These are the things I find in odd or scary sites that *aren't* haunted

You'll learn to find logical, *non*-ghostly explanations for what's happening in your home... and how to fix it.

But if you DO have a ghost (or two or three)...

After you've ruled out normal issues, if the problems continue, I'll explain some of your options.

If it's ghostly *energy,* not an actual ghost (I'll explain the difference, later), I'll share tips that may help you reduce or banish it.

If it's an *actual* ghost that's lost and confused, I'll describe ways you can help it "cross over."

And, if it's one of those rare territorial – or even malicious – entities, I'll describe some of the best ways to protect yourself and your family.

You're about to learn what we know about ghosts: What they are. What they aren't. And what to do if your home *is* haunted.

Let's get started.

1

Safety First - The Fatal Four

Some "haunted" houses are dangerous... but for *normal* reasons. They may contain carbon monoxide, damaged electrical wiring, uneven floors and stairways, and residents may struggle with sleep interruptions.

Every one of these can explain things we often associate with haunted houses, so let's address them first. This could – literally – save your life.

Carbon monoxide

Carbon monoxide is nicknamed "the silent killer." Pets and children often react to it first.

Carbon monoxide (CO), also called carbonous oxide, is a colorless, odorless, and tasteless gas.

In high quantities, it can make humans and animals ill or even kill them.

Here's how Wikipedia described the problem: *"The most common symptoms of carbon monoxide poisoning may resemble other types of poisonings and infections, including symptoms such as **headache, nausea, vomiting, dizziness, fatigue and a feeling of weakness. Infants may be irritable and feed poorly. Neurological signs include confusion, disorientation, visual disturbance, syncope, and seizures."***

Carbon monoxide can come from various sources, including gas appliances, wood stoves, car exhaust, blocked flues, and cigarette smoke.

Many UK, American, and Canadian areas have laws recommending (or even requiring) carbon monoxide detectors in homes. (Older landlords or homeowners may not realize that.)

Even if your home does not have a fireplace or wood stove and no gas appliances, *check the levels anyway.*

For example, if a nearby neighbor has a wood stove, smoke may drift into your home, even if you keep your windows closed.

[Tip for professionals: If you regularly investigate haunted sites, be sure *your* home has very low levels of carbon monoxide, too. If you've been sensitized to the gas, even low levels might trigger your symptoms at a "haunted" site. Or, if you've been living with low-level symptoms daily, you might not realize their effects on you.]

How to check for it

If you (or the landlord or homeowner) don't have a carbon monoxide detector installed and you don't have a handheld monitor, visit your local hardware or DIY store. Some carbon monoxide detectors are very affordable. After all, this really *is* a matter of life or death.

Or, call the fire department for advice. Some fire departments provide carbon monoxide detectors free of charge.

Exposed or damaged electrical wiring

Electromagnetic fields (EMF) occur in everyone's house. In today's device-dependent world, elevated EMF levels are normal. (They don't tell you this on most ghost-related TV shows.)

However, unusually *high* levels of EMF energy can be a health risk, and it's easily overlooked.

EMF can be related to the wiring in your house and how well it's shielded.

You may also experience higher EMF around a TV, computer monitor, or microwave oven. As long as the EMF is within safe levels and you don't spend much time near it, that's fine.

Well, maybe. Some people are electrosensitive. (The World Health Organization is studying this. More research is needed.)

High EMF levels in any part of your home can cause problems. It explains why some people *think* their homes are haunted, when they're not.

In at least 70% of the homes I've investigated, where the homeowner complained about a haunted basement, the problem

was old wiring. That's so routine that I check it first when someone complains about "feeling weird" in the basement or an area close to the basement stairs.

Here are the symptoms of EMF sensitivity:
- skin redness, tingling, or a burning sensation
- fatigue
- concentration difficulties
- dizziness
- nausea
- heart palpitation
- digestive disturbances

Some people also report anxiety, insomnia, and memory loss. Others report symptoms ranging from abdominal pain to hallucinations.

How to check for it

EMF levels are measured with an EMF detector. (Note: Ghost-hunting EMF tools often have very different sensitivities when compared with DIY stores' EMF meters. Start with an inexpensive EMF meter from a DIY or hardware store.)

You *can* check EMF levels yourself, but you should probably consult a professional. If the EMF levels are constantly high, fix the problem immediately.

Then, re-evaluate your ghost evidence.

Uneven floors & stairways

When someone thinks a stairway is haunted, check it immediately. This is especially true if older adults or very young children use those stairs regularly.

About 30% of the time, when someone reports a haunted stairway, one or more treads (steps) are slightly tilted. Check if it's slanted from side to side. Also, check from front to back.

How to check for this

You'll need a simple, inexpensive carpenter's level, usually less than $10, in a DIY store. It can show if a floor, window frame, door frame, or stairs are uneven. Check several spots on each stair step. One side might be fine, but another could be skewed.

If just one step in a stairway is tilted, even a little, people can feel uneasy on those stairs.

If a staircase still seems haunted, measure the angle *and* height of *each* step. Even a ¼ inch difference can cause some people to lose their footing or feel pushed on those stairs.

However, it's not just stairways that can disorient a person or cause physical, ghost-like phenomena.

A poorly made house or an older, settled home can be out of alignment. That's normal, especially when the home is built on sandy or moist soil.

If floors are at a slight angle, they can trigger low-level anxiety or cause physical phenomena.

Also, use a carpenter's level to check any doors and furniture drawers that seem to open or close by themselves, even when no one is near them.

Sleep interruptions

In increasing numbers, people are reporting terrible nightmares and being woken by a creature (usually hideous) that prevents them from moving or even breathing.

There are several clinical terms for this. They include sleep paralysis, night terrors, and "old hag syndrome."

It's normal. Most people will experience it three or four times in their lifetime. Few forget the experience.

But, if this happens regularly, it can be *very* dangerous.

Interrupted sleep – whether from a normal or *para*normal problem – can cause mental and physical health issues. Left untreated, they can become life-threatening.

First, talk with a sleep doctor. They might suggest eliminating all light sources inside your bedroom, even your digital clock. You may need to adjust the temperature in your bedroom or use earplugs to reduce noise. Also, you should be checked for sleep apnea.

Many of these terrifying encounters can be prevented. Often, they're caused by a combination of devices emitting low-level EMF; you can fix this *right now*.

What to do, right now

First, remove all electrical devices – phones, radios, remote controls, alarm clocks, laptops, phone chargers, and even lights – from the nightstand or any surface in or near the bed.

Turn off the phone, and move all electrical devices at least five or six feet away from the bed.

If the problem continues, try putting the devices in another room altogether.

Unless you have a medical reason to wear a watch or sleep-monitoring device when you're in bed, consider sleeping without it for a few nights and see if that helps. (Do *not* stop using devices that doctors have prescribed or suggested. However, make an appointment to discuss your sleep problems with them, if the interruptions continue.)

Wifi signals, etc., may be part of the problem. Ask your doctor about that possibility.

Most persistent cases of sleep paralysis resolve with the steps outlined above.

After two or three weeks of getting the nightly sleep you need, you may feel surprisingly better and never encounter "old hag syndrome" again.

If you *still* experience nightly disturbances, use an EMF meter to measure potentially high electromagnetic fields around your bed and bedroom, or wherever you sleep.

If you discover high EMF levels, contact an electrician to help with wiring or at least create a buffer around your bed.

While discussing the most common complaints about "haunted" houses, the following are not as dangerous but can – and should – be checked.

Haunted doors, cabinets, drawers, and windows

These issues are rarely dangerous, but most are easily identified with a carpenter's level.

Doors, cabinets, and drawers that open or close when no one is nearby

Many tenants worry that ghosts are opening or closing doors, cabinets, and drawers. If that's the *only* symptom of a haunting, it's probably a structural issue.

If a door frame has sagged with age, that could explain door problems.

That's true of any wooden feature in your home.

First, check the door, cabinet, or drawer – and its frame – with the carpenter's level.

Then, see if you can "debunk" the problem by walking heavily in another part of the room.

Check if the door opens or closes too easily – or even by itself – when a different (usually exterior) door is opened or closed. That can affect the air pressure inside the house, especially in homes that have been super-insulated or otherwise made relatively airtight.

In rare cases, the home's forced-air heating or cooling system can cause doors to drift closed, or pop open by themselves.

Windows that open or close by themselves

Windows can have structural issues, too, but they're infrequently reported as "a ghost."

A loose window *can* close itself. I've seen that many times, and it can be dangerous. However, double-hung windows rarely *open* on their own, unless the counterweight is too heavy.

Window *shades* can snap or unroll when the winding mechanism is too tight or loose. You may need to replace the shades.

Though these aren't the only normal (or normal-ish) explanations for ghostly activity in a home, they are the most common.

With those critical safety issues addressed, it's time to examine ghosts and haunted sites in more detail.

2

Get the Most From This Book

If you're living in – or investigating – a house that *seems* haunted, start at the beginning of this book. Work your way through it, step by step.

First, rule out *normal* explanations. It can take just a few days to determine if the house is haunted – or just *seems* like it is.

Often, you can debunk – and fix – whatever the problem is.

Sometimes it's better to consult a professional.

Be patient. It might take weeks (or longer) to determine what's really going on.

> If – at *any* time – you feel as if you're at risk, <u>leave the house immediately</u>. If the problem might be a *structural* safety risk, like a gas leak or bad household wiring, contact a professional repair service. If you're fairly certain the issue is ghostly or possibly demonic, talk with a trusted priest, minister, or spiritual counselor in your community. This should be someone you know in real life, *and trust.* Follow their guidance.

Assuming you're at least comfortable in your home (most of the time, anyway), you'll start by looking for normal answers to what's happening. They're in the first part of this book.

After "debunking" your home, if it *still* seems haunted or has an *odd* energy, you'll explore the next section.

By completing all the steps in this book, you should feel confident about what is – and isn't – going on at the house you're investigating.

If you still have questions, the answers may be in the Appendix section at the back of this book. Though most homeowners won't need that information, it can be useful for specialized situations.

For more information about ghosts, see my other books, my website, HollowHill.com, and my YouTube channel, youtube.com/@fionab roome.

3

First, Keep a Diary

No one can tell you whether or not a house is truly haunted.

However, by eliminating all natural explanations for what you're experiencing, you can decide whether or not the house probably has a ghost, or even several entities.

Ruling out what's normal (and can be fixed) is always your first step when a house might be haunted.

First, keep a diary of your experiences in the house.

Keep a diary of what seems to be going on in the house. (If you're investigating for a tenant, have them keep this kind of diary, too.)

It can be a simple, spiral-bound notebook or some sheets of paper. Or, you can use something like my "Is Your House Haunted?" journal, but – really – this step just requires you to take notes.

Every time you think you might be encountering a ghost, write down everything about it, including how you feel about it.

Note the date, time, and weather conditions.

Write down who's in the house with you. Include what you're experiencing, including things you see, hear, smell, or feel, and any odd tastes you notice in your mouth.

At first, include every possible detail. Did you eat recently, and what was it? Had anyone expressed strong emotions (positive or negative) right before the incident?

Take photos if you can, and include prints of them in your diary.

See if you can find any pattern to what's going on, such as a time, day of the week or month, or something about the weather.

Keep this for at least four or five encounters, or until you see a clear pattern – whichever comes first.

You're doing this so you know exactly when the odd events are most likely to happen. It may lead to a simple explanation. Many of them are covered in this book.

When the answer isn't simple

In some cases, the issue may require a more professional evaluation. If so, arrange for the repair person to be in the house when whatever-it-is happens.

In most cases, professionals must be able to witness the phenomena. Then they can tell you if there's a normal explanation... or if dealing with the issue – such as a ghost – is outside their expertise.

It's a lot like taking your car to a mechanic. Unless they can hear the noise (or whatever the problem is), they can't diagnose what's causing it.

The more information you gather ahead of time, the better your chances of quickly identifying what's causing the problem.

And, if you see no activity pattern at all, a professional can ask you additional questions that narrow the possible explanations.

For example, in the autumn – around Halloween – people often turn on the heat in their homes.

After a couple of weeks, the wood in the house can dry out, and shrink slightly. This can cause doors to pop open by themselves, floors to creak, and other physical phenomena.

A handyman or home heating expert may be able to tell you if that explains your ghostly experiences.

Here's a sample entry in a diary at a haunted house.

Date: Wednesday, October 9th, 2024
 Time: 10:00 p.m. to about 11:25 p.m.
 Weather: Rainy night, windy, no moon.
 Who was there: I was at home, alone.
 What happened: I was in the kitchen, feeling happy as I prepared a snack. Then, I heard a moaning sound coming from the attic. It was slow and muffled. There was a smell like pipe smoke, too.
 I felt startled, but not scared.
 When I turned on the attic light, the noise stopped, and the smell went away quickly. There was no a/c in the attic, and the windows were locked shut.

I checked the entire attic, and there was no smoke. The attic smoke detector was still working okay.

When I returned to the kitchen, my left shoulder ached, and I felt sad for no reason.

About ten minutes later, the sound in the attic started again. The aroma of pipe smoke didn't return.

The noise stopped just before 11:30 p.m., but I still felt a little sad and unsettled by what was going on.

This morning, my shoulder feels fine, and the sadness is gone. However, I still feel uneasy about what I experienced. I also have the oddest feeling that I must be wary of my next-door neighbor. The weird thing is, that house is empty. It's for sale, and no one has lived there for months.

4

A Leading Culprit: Mold, Mildew, and Allergens

Are you sensitive to or allergic to something in the house? Even subtle levels of mold or mildew can trigger headaches or anxiety in some people.

Also, allergies to paints, new carpeting, cleaning products, or air fresheners can lead to symptoms of physical and emotional stress.

Several allergy symptoms and reactions can mimic what some people experience at haunted sites. They include:

- Tingling, especially around the mouth, lips, or throat.
- Numbness in the extremities. (Rare.)
- Cough, chest tightness, and airway swelling can block breathing.
- Light-headedness, feeling faint, or loss of consciousness.
- Shortness of breath and a rapid, weak pulse.
- Nausea and vomiting

Especially if the house suddenly seems haunted, *look for what's changed.* Review new (or overdue) home improvements, new cleaning products, or new furnishings.

Cut flowers or a garden outside your window can trigger new and seasonal allergies. People usually know if they have hay fever. However, if the symptoms are minor, they can be invisible factors in things like headaches and "weeping" eyes. Apps are available to tell you which allergens are currently in season.

Wood smoke can be another seasonal allergen. Many "haunted" fireplaces are the result of built-up smoke residue and are witnessed only by people who are sensitive to it. Also, see if any neighbors are using a wood stove or their fireplaces or if they've been burning leaves or trash in their yards.

Another culprit can be a neglected HVAC system, with dust or mildew inside, leading to physical complaints. You may need a professional evaluation to check that, but a simple visual check might reveal neglected ducts.

Well-worn carpets may also hold allergens, or mildew might be beneath them. That may require a professional cleaning service. (In some cases, when carpeting or pads are replaced, people feel less anxious or on-edge, in the house.)

Likewise, sensitivity to mold and mildew may explain why some people feel very uncomfortable in their home's basement. But remember, chemicals that remove mold and mildew can also produce fumes. If you or visitors are already sensitized to odors, they may need to stay away from the home during – and immediately after – the cleaning.

In new homes, a good dehumidifier can prevent mold and mildew in basements. (Elevated EMF is another likely issue in a basement, particularly around fuse boxes and wiring. You may be able to diagnose that with an inexpensive EMF meter from your local DIY store.)

If mold, mildew, or allergies might be part of the problem, consult a professional. Their advice may help you relieve the "haunted" sensations in the house and save on medical bills, too.

5

Animals in The Walls, Chimney, or Attic

Your "ghost" might be an animal or a nest of animals. This is more common than you may realize.

"Ghostly" sounds from animals can include:

• Scratching or fluttering noises, or the tapping sound like little feet running nearby.

• Sounds like whispering or even light laughter.

• Crying or chattering of baby animals in a nest.

• Whimpering, calling, and moaning of a trapped animal or an animal in heat.

You or a local home repair professional can look for signs of animal visitors. These include droppings or remnants of food, scratch marks, nesting materials, etc.

Don't overlook the chimney, attic, crawlspaces, and basement. Although the animal may *seem* to be in your walls or HVAC ducts, it may enter or exit through an opening somewhere else in the house... or outside it.

Check both the inside and outside of your home, including the roof and eaves of your home.

You may need an inspection by someone who specializes in pest issues. Your town or county may have an animal control office, which may provide that service free of charge.

Mice, squirrels, and raccoons are frequent culprits, but they're not the only ones. The hum of a beehive or a wasp's nest – muffled by walls and insulation – can create weird vibrations and humming sounds. (Remember, some critters are nocturnal, so you'll only sense them at night.)

In warmer climates, giant insects – such as palmetto bugs – can create startling noises inside your walls, HVAC ducts, or floors.

Detection can be tricky, so if you can't diagnose or resolve the problem on your own, it's wise to seek help from local resources.

6

Plumbing, Heating, and A/C Noises Can Fool You

If you've recently moved into a home with steam or hot water heat, noises in the pipes may surprise you. They can sound like moaning, whistling, whispering, humming, or something pounding on the floor or walls.

Start by asking former residents or visitors, "Have you heard any odd noises from the pipes, or anything else I should know about?"

Air pockets in your plumbing can sound eerie immediately after pipes are worked on, including work on water mains in your neighborhood.

(You've probably seen your faucet shudder and clang when you first run the water after an outage or repair. You'd never confuse that with anything paranormal. However, lesser after-effects can be more challenging to recognize.)

Also, a furnace or air conditioning system can make strange noises when it needs maintenance.

If you've used something to increase or decrease the humidity in your home or basement, check that device for mold or mildew, too. Many devices have filters that need to be cleaned or replaced regularly.

An odorless carbon monoxide leak from your furnace can cause symptoms that mimic a haunting.

If you suspect this, check those levels right now. Carbon monoxide can kill you! If you're not ready to invest in a carbon monoxide detector – or you're not sure if yours is still working – call a professional. (Your fire department or county extension office may offer this service, perhaps free of charge.)

Take no chances.

Also, check your gas-fired water heater for related problems.

If you use window air conditioning units or swamp coolers, know where excess moisture drains. Dripping or trickling water can make odd noises.

Older heating systems, especially steam heat, can explain seasonal thumps and banging noises. If your household hot water runs from or through your furnace, that issue can be a year-round problem.

A pro can tell you immediately if a particular noise could be caused by plumbing, heating, or a/c issues. All it may take is a phone call to identify a normal source of "ghostly" sounds and vibrations.

7

Drafts, Rumbles, and Underground Water

Unusual – but normal – conditions can make a home seem haunted. Some of them are so simple that they're easily overlooked.

When doors "close by themselves," or light objects move when no one is near, suspect a draft.

You or your home handyperson can check for drafts, usually with a candle. (If the draft is strong but intermittent, please use care!)

Heavier objects can seem to move by themselves if a train or heavy truck passes nearby, particularly if your floor or surface isn't level. Note the exact times when this happens; it may fit a regular transport schedule or one recently altered.

Also, if subtle vibrations from a train, truck, or underground stream are involved, you can run a preliminary check with a glass of water. (This is similar to what was shown in the movie *Jurassic Park*.)

Some people – especially those with inner ear sensitivities – can become disoriented near very low frequencies generated by underground streams.

Those noises are often below a level that people notice on a conscious level, but they still affect us. They're called infrasound. At least 30% of "haunted" houses I've investigated may have seemed more intense due to infrasound.

(In fact, whenever I watch a ghost-related TV show, and the possibly haunted house is near a river, stream, or bridge, I don't take seriously any "yes, it's a ghost" conclusions. It's too easy for producers to overlook an obvious answer – like infrasound – for the sake of a compelling episode.)

A geological map may help identify underground water sources beneath or near your home. A surprising number of convincing, ghostly phenomena have occurred over or near underground streams and near ponds, waterfalls, dams, and rivers. Infrasound *may* be related.

Infrasound can lead to stress in some people. In fact, the "dark history" of many haunted homes may be rooted in infrasound and its effects on past tenants or visitors.

You may need to move if infrasound is involved and the problem is severe. But, from my experience, most people simply need an answer to what's happening in their homes. Once they can say, "Oh, it's just that river a few blocks away," that reduces their anxieties, and they can remain in their homes happily.

Here's some trivia: Water is implicated in *other* ways at haunted houses. Scientists are still studying the relationship between water and paranormal activity. (See the EIFs article near the back of this book.)

Unexplained water is another separate, quirky, paranormal issue. It's been observed at sites like California's Winchester mansion.

Also, water is often associated with poltergeist activity, including objects that seem to move – sometimes across a room – by themselves. At least 90% of poltergeist activity reported to me has occurred near water (bathroom, kitchen, or a fish tank), or people have reported small, nearby areas of unexplained water. The latter are usually the size of dimes, nickels, and quarters. I will talk about this in a later chapter.

8

Trapped in Bed?

If you are troubled by ghosts when you sleep, it may be "sleep paralysis."

Many people experience this at least once or twice in their lifetimes. It's normal, but it can be scary at the time.

It feels as if you are awake (or trying to wake up), and someone or something is holding you down. Maybe you can't breathe, swallow, or even move a muscle.

You may feel certain that the entity is across the room, next to your bed, or even sitting on your chest or back.

Some people see an entity. It's usually an ugly older woman, a man in rags, a very evil-looking entity, or some demon. (In the past, sleep paralysis has been called "old hag syndrome.")

Another variation: you may feel as if you're levitating, either inside or outside your body, and floating above your bed.

No matter how this manifests, people usually feel fully awake – and alarmed – when they experience it. It can be nearly impossible to convince them that the experience *wasn't* caused by a ghost or demonic entity.

According to a Penn State professor, Brian Sharpless, nearly 8% of the general population and 28% of college students will experience (and remember) symptoms of sleep paralysis. The numbers are higher if you already experience panic disorders.

If this happens more than twice a month, ask your doctor for advice. Rule out health issues immediately. Your doctor may suggest a sleep aid to help break unconscious habits that trigger these terrifying experiences.

Stress and sleep loss can trigger repeated events. To prevent future sleep disturbances, you may need a few nights of good, uninterrupted REM (rapid eye movement) sleep.

(Some people explain sleep paralysis as what happens when you're woken from deep REM sleep, but the natural – and light – paralysis of REM hasn't worn off yet. If these are rare occasions, that may be the answer. You may have been woken by a neighbor's late-night party, a heavy truck going past your home, or some other unusual cause.)

If the problem continues, consult a sleep specialist, even if you're *sure* it's a ghost. In some cases, sleep paralysis can be related to sleep apnea, a potentially dangerous health condition. So, if these night-time disturbances occur several times, talk with a doctor *immediately*.

However, if the disturbances continue and your doctor is certain there's no *physical* reason for your experiences, set boundaries with your ghosts. Tell them – out loud – to leave you alone at night.

If that fails, folk remedies include placing a bowl of salt on your nightstand. Almost 100% of the people who try it report that it solves or at least reduces the problem within three nights.

9

No Normal Answers?

If you still can't discover a *normal* explanation for what you're experiencing, your house *might* be haunted.

Of course, get a second opinion from a home inspector or repair person.

You don't need to raise the issue of ghosts. It may be better if you don't. Just describe what's going on.

Also, see if a neighbor knows what's causing odd phenomena in your home. For example, if squirrels are getting into a neighbor's attic, that might also explain odd noises in your attic.

In addition, if a home was built near yours recently – or if someone put in a new well – they may know about underground springs and streams in the area. The infrasound issues can be very subtle, so the more insights you can gather, the better.

Who built your home? Often, that same carpenter or contractors built neighboring houses, too. If so, a neighbor may already know about uneven floors, irregular stairways, EMF issues with wiring, or mold in vents around the attic.

Shabby quality is more common than you might expect.

Environmental factors such as extreme, drying heat, heavy rain, or earth tremors and earthquakes – recent ones or from decades ago – may have affected the structure of your home, as well. Check historical records at your town hall or public library, and chat with local historians and folklore experts. Their stories may include valuable insights.

For now, if the situation is annoying but not scary, continue to keep your diary of what happens and when. Maybe you need more evidence. A pattern of activity can point to non-ghostly answers... or indicate an actual haunting. (Remember: 80% of the "haunted" homes that I investigate *are not haunted.)*

For example, someone might be playing a prank. It's rare, but it happens. If the problem is a prankster, they will get tired of it, especially if it looks like you're not frightened.

No matter the explanation, it's vital to have someone – like a home inspector – witness, or at least investigate, what's happening. That may be the only way you'll know if there's a normal (and fixable) reason for what you're experiencing.

In addition, you may need to consult a home construction expert – someone with extensive professional experience – to rule out all normal possibilities. Ask neighbors to recommend companies they've used in the past.

But, because you are vulnerable when stressed or frightened, ask for references before bringing anyone into your home. Check online reviews. Ask friends if they've heard anything about the company or individual.

When the professional or team arrives for the inspection, you may learn some helpful (and money-saving) tips about maintaining your home. If they have to fix something, always ask, "What can I do to prevent this in the future?"

On the other hand...

Let's say *no one* – even experts – can explain what's happening in your home. With everything *normal* ruled out, the answer may be *paranormal*. If so, it's time to take your research to the next level.

Please keep safety in mind. Some paranormal activity can be dangerous. Take no risks.

Are you or your family members extremely stressed or losing sleep? Is your ghost affecting your daily life? Get help from your doctor or a member of your *local* religious community, not from a stranger online. Do this *immediately*.

If that's not helpful or practical, stay with friends or family (or even at a local motel) until you're refreshed and ready to deal with this again.

If you have children and they're affected – directly or indirectly – perhaps they can stay with grandparents while you resolve this. It's <u>vital</u> to prevent childhood trauma that might occur from the events in your home.

So, assuming that you've exhausted all normal explanations, *and* if this is a low-level (but odd) and unresolved problem in your home, a paranormal approach may help.

Don't panic at the word "paranormal." That doesn't mean it's dangerous. Most hauntings present no risks once you know what's going on. But, just in case, take every precaution that you can, not just for yourself but for those close to you, as well.

10

What to Do If It Might Be a Ghost

If you feel fairly certain that your house is haunted, it's time to decide how serious the problem is.

First, consider the risks – physical, emotional, and spiritual – and their effects on the people who live in and visit your home.

In most cases, the haunting isn't the most significant problem... it's how people *react* to the idea that a ghost (or even a demon) might be nearby.

That anxiety and fear can spiral into something dangerous for *everyone* involved.

This is worth repeating: If you or your family feel like you're in danger, get out of the house.

Even if your fears seem silly, don't stay there. Visit friends or neighbors, or stay at a nearby bed and breakfast or motel.

After a few days, you may feel confident enough to return to your home and start the next steps. (However, if a demon or evil entity might be involved, get help, and stay away from the house until you're confident that it's cleared.)

Next, assuming the problem is annoying instead of terrifying, it's time to take the next steps.

Once you've ruled out normal explanations, it's important to identify the *kind* of haunting (or hauntings) you're dealing with.

Rarely, multiple ghosts linger at some locations. But your home can also seem (or be) haunted *without* having a ghost or any other entity.

Does that surprise you? Well, it's more common than you might realize, and it's an issue we'll address first.

It's called a "residual energy haunting."

It's not dangerous, but it can be unsettling to live with until you find a way to control or eliminate it.

That's what we'll talk about in the next chapter.

11

When Weird Things Happen, Regularly

Residual energy hauntings seem to be leftover energy, after one or more intensely emotional events at the site.

It's like walking into a room after two people have had an ugly argument. You can almost *feel* the crackle of energy in the air.

Similarly, energy can linger after any dramatic event in your house, even something that happened decades ago.

It could be something tragic, such as a death or a broken heart. Perhaps mournful energy seems to be embedded in the walls.

Or, it could be energy lingering after a series of birthday parties, or dinner parties that included the most powerful people in town.

This is where your diary can be helpful. You're looking for *repeating* "ghostly" activity – usually an *ambiance* - and what might trigger it.

It might be an odd reaction – something physical or something you sense – every time you re-watch a classic movie, play a classic "oldies" album, or when the national anthem is played at the start of a sports event you're watching on TV or online.

It could recur on the 12th day of every month, every time a certain friend or relative drops by for a visit, or every time you bake cookies.

As long as it's just odd, not scary, you may be able to reduce or even eliminate it.

Reminder: If – at *any* time – you feel in danger, leave the house immediately. Don't return to the house alone if you feel especially at risk. Talk with a local priest or trusted spiritual minister about what's happening. To the best of our knowledge, ghosts cannot seriously injure you or kill you, but other entities might. (And yes, I'll repeat this warning throughout this book. It's that important.)

Assuming that the ghost-like activity is minor, here's one way to determine if an *actual* ghost is involved: Try to recreate whatever pattern you've noticed in connection with it. See if whatever-it-is – the ghost-like phenomena – happens again. And then get it to repeat in a simple cause-and-effect style.

If it does, at least some of the "hauntings" at your home are residual energy.

If recreating triggers doesn't work, or you *can't* recreate them for some logistical reason, you can try the opposite approach.

See if you can nudge the ghost (if there is one) to respond.

Turn lights on and off. Randomly open and close doors and windows. Talk to the ghost as if you know it's there. Generally, shake up the energy in the house.

If you get a reaction, stop immediately. You probably have your answer: It's an entity, and possibly a ghost.

In that case, do *not* antagonize whatever the entity is. Skip ahead to the "Helpful Spirits" chapter.

WARNING: Do not use a Ouija board or anything occult. Don't attempt a seance or automatic writing. Don't try to "channel" the ghost – or do anything that allows the spirit to use your body (or your hands, etc.) – to speak *through* you. Don't try to copy something you saw on TV, either.

However, if nothing changes, no matter what you do, it could be residual energy. You just haven't identified what triggers it, yet.

I say "could be," because it *might* still be a ghost, but – at the moment – it simply isn't interested in responding.

Or, you might also have a ghost (or ghosts) and residual energy. But let's say that it's just residual energy, not a ghost. In some cases, you can reduce the residual energy.

In others, you can't. (I have no idea why. There haven't been enough repeatable, scientific tests to prove *any* of this. We're basing our advice on past experience in this field.)

The classic way to handle residual energy – and it can help with *some* annoying ghosts – is called "space clearing." It seems to reduce the lingering, residual energy.

You can do this with a blessing, another prayer, or a benign ritual that fits your spirituality.

Or, you can use non-religious methods based on folklore, such as walking around the room (or house) and waving incense. Usually, a sage smudge works best for this; you can either make one yourself or buy one from almost any New Age or health food retailer, online or offline.

However, my favorite technique is to use a vacuum cleaner in the room – or rooms – where the hauntings seem to occur. Vacuum clean every square inch of the room, including the floor, walls, and ceiling. Spend extra time vacuum cleaning corners, especially high up. (You'll need a wand-style attachment for this.)

Some people think electricity banishes the residual energy. Others believe it's the noise. So, the noisier the vacuum cleaner, the better.

You may need to repeat this several times. If it doesn't work within a week or two, try different space-clearing techniques. I describe them in the next chapter.

In most cases, you can *reduce* the residual energy but not entirely remove it. Often, some of that energy must dissipate on its own. This can take days or years, depending on what triggers the energy, and how much it seems to be *re*charging from the environment.

Remember that residual energy does *not* involve an entity. No matter how that residual energy affects you emotionally or physically, that energy is not a ghost or a demon. You are not at risk from residual energy.

Some research suggests that many – even *most* – hauntings might be the result of residual energy. (I'm not making that claim; I'm just noting it. I haven't enough proof to be certain.)

In my opinion, residual energy is merely annoying, and – with patience - it can usually be reduced or eliminated.

And, if not, you may get used to it, or even forget that it's there.

12

More Space Clearing Methods

Space clearing has been used for centuries to improve – or unblock – helpful energy in homes and businesses. This isn't necessarily religious, though many people consider it "New Age."

If you're uncomfortable with space-clearing techniques, skip them. Ask your local, trusted priest, minister, rabbi, bishop, or spiritual advisor for help.

Dealing with unknown spiritual matters, *never try something that bothers you*. If you're uneasy, there are always different ways to deal with the issue. (Doing something that makes you mentally, emotionally, or spiritually uncomfortable could open the door to opportunistic issues. Don't risk that.)

But let's say you're comfortable with folklore-based space-clearing techniques.

Vacuuming (mentioned in the last chapter) is a relatively new method. Other approaches have been used successfully in various cultures and eras.

Start with what's easy. If that doesn't work, try something else.

Music

Many people believe that music heals individuals and clears the air. Play happy, upbeat, or deeply spiritual music. Sing along, tap your feet, clap, and contribute your own energy to the power of the music.

In most cases, 20 - 30 minutes of music (a single album) will tell you if this technique might work for your space.

Live music can work, too. If all else fails, singing "For He's a Jolly Good Fellow" – over and over again while you clean house – can be enough.

If you'd like an aerobic workout, put on your favorite, lively music and dance or exercise in the room with the issues.

(However, if there is *any* possibility that a malicious entity might be involved, do *not* conduct drumming... not even a drumming circle with friends. Drumming puts some people in a trance state, and that leaves some of them vulnerable. Though the chances of that are very slim, keep them in mind.)

Another warning: Don't whistle. In many cultures, worldwide, people believe whistling attracts bad luck or evil spirits. (I'm not sure whether to take that seriously and – since I can't seem to whistle – I can't speak from experience.)

Incense

Many people like to use incense or a sage "smudge." Incense has been used since antiquity to banish bad smells and insects. According to folklore, it will also banish bad energy (including residual energy hauntings).

Light the incense. Wave it around each affected room. Don't create so much smoke that you're choking, but it should be enough to set off your smoke detector. (You may want to turn off any detectors in or near the room, but only if you're sure you'll remain safe, and only until the smoke dissipates.) On the other hand, some people carry a glass of water in case an ember flies off the incense and creates a fire hazard. As they say: better safe than sorry!

Spread the smoky aroma throughout the room. That's all you need to do.

Generally, people believe that smoke helps, partly due to the particles released into the air. In other words, an air freshener may not be a good substitute.

Singing bowls and other noisemakers

Other people use a "singing bowl." I own and use one, even before trying the vacuum cleaner approach.

Ring the bowl throughout the haunted room/s until the tone carries clearly. (Haunted areas tend to muffle the sound. Once the sound seems normal, that area is clear. Move to the next area.)

Likewise, wind chimes are supposed to clear out bad energy and evil spirits.

Bells can be a substitute, too.

(Trivia: In the Middle Ages, the Catholic Church recommended bells to frighten away evil spirits. The old expression "ring out your dead" was about ringing a bell around the dead – corpses and graves, alike - to keep evil spirits away from the bodies.)

No matter what noisemaker you use, make sure the sound is loud and clear, and carries throughout the room you're clearing.

For more space-clearing ideas, see the Feng Shui section at the back of this book.

If space clearing doesn't help – or even makes things worse – you may have an actual ghost or other entity. Some of them seem to hate noise unless they cause it.

If space clearing worsens things, expect annoying phenomena for about three days. Usually, when things settle down again, they're better than before the space clearing was tried.

However, don't rely on music, incense, bells, or any space-clearing technique if the situation is dangerous.

At the other extreme, if a child is unreasonably afraid of imagined ghosts, using a bell or wind chime – with an explanation of related centuries-old traditions – might be all you need to banish their fears. Sure, it's a placebo, but sometimes simple methods can calm a child's fears about monsters under the bed or ghosts in the closet.

13

Helpful Spirits

Is your ghost a helpful or benevolent spirit?

In some – perhaps many – cases, houses are "haunted" by loving, caring spirits.

Too often, people think of ghosts the way they're represented in scary movies and TV shows.

Yes, some ghosts can seem misguided, malicious, or territorial. However, there are no "killer ghosts" stalking your home with butcher knives.

In fact, your "ghost" may be the spirit of a family member who is there to help and support you. They may even protect you from danger.

Or, your ghost may be a former resident (or residents) who liked your home so well, they return to it regularly. (I'm reminded of the TV series, "Ghosts.") If you research the history of your home, you may identify them. That can make the spirits seem less frightening.

If your ghost doesn't want to leave, don't insist on it. That's rude and – frankly – not very fair, either.

You can find ways to live together.

You may have to set "ground rules" to co-exist with your ghost (or ghosts).

For example, you could talk out loud to your ghost or ghosts. Act as if they are physically there. Explain the problem and the best solution. Ask the ghosts to respect your rules and your boundaries.

For example, it's unacceptable for them to scare you or others, or to interrupt your sleep. Pranks are not allowed, especially around stairways, electrical appliances, and anything involving heat, like a stove or iron.

Note: Ghosts *can* be forgetful or mischievous. You may need to repeat the rules several times.

However, many people think of their ghosts as invisible room-mates... who don't leave the toilet seat up or steal your food from the refrigerator.

There are stories about lives (and houses) saved through the *help* of a resident ghost. (She's usually a ghostly woman dressed in green.)

Most people find ways to live comfortably with ghosts in their homes.

If the ghosts are respectful, you can live together in the same house.

At the other extreme, some people treat ghosts as pets, performers, or property of the homeowner.

Don't expect your ghost to perform on demand. It's not fair to try to contain or restrict your ghost's freedom, either. You don't "own" the ghost, and even – or especially – the ghost of a child should never be treated like your personal property.

Spirits must be allowed free will, as long as they aren't causing problems in your daily life.

14

Inconsiderate Ghosts

Some ghosts aren't mean or dangerous. They're just annoying. Some don't understand boundaries, either.

They wake you with noises at night. They chill the room on winter nights. They frighten your pets or your nervous grandmother.

If that's what you're dealing with, talk out loud with your ghost. Tell it *exactly* what's upsetting you, and why. A simple, "Stop that!" may not be enough.

Remember, *a ghost is still a person.*

If they don't respond well – or keep "forgetting" the rules – you may need to be more assertive. (In one haunted house I lived in, one of our ghosts didn't like electrical lights. So, when all else failed, and it misbehaved, I'd leave a few lights on 24/7. It worked, at least three or four days at a time.)

But, before taking further steps, always explain – out loud – to your ghost why those penalties are necessary.

If your ghost is a joker or merely difficult to live with, it's not time for an exorcism.

Lesser folk remedies may help you and your ghost co-exist happily, or encourage the ghost to leave.

Many of these remedies sound silly and don't make much sense to us. However, these solutions have worked for hundreds of years. We don't know – and don't need to know – why they're effective.

In the next few sections, I'll talk about classic and folklore-based cures for problem ghosts.

Note: If you're uncomfortable with any of these techniques, talk with your priest, minister, or other spiritual advisor. Never use tactics or practices that make you uneasy. (That's not because the practices are dangerous, but because it's a spiritual compromise for you. That path can lead to danger.)

15

Folklore - Shoes and Rice

Ghosts have been documented almost as long as there's been written history.

Successful cures have also been recorded, often in folklore. Some of them work remarkably well, even in the most haunted homes.

The shoe cure

One of the simplest, silliest cures is to take two shoes and turn them side-by-side so their respective toes point in opposite directions.

Then, leave them there.

According to folklore, this confuses the ghosts, who'll stare at the shoes all night.

I successfully used this at the very haunted Myrtles Plantation in Louisiana.

During a late night in one of the house's most haunted bedrooms, I was ready for sleep. I'd already talked and complained to the ghosts about keeping me awake when I needed sleep. The turned-around shoes bought me about 20 minutes of peace for a quick nap. (I wouldn't have believed this if I hadn't seen it work, myself. Since then, many HollowHill.com readers have said it works for them, too.)

The rice cure

A similar "cure" is to throw a handful of rice on the floor in the room where the ghost is most active. (If you have a choice, the kitchen is usually recommended.) Folklore claims that ghosts will compulsively count the grains over & over again and – because they're so busy counting – they'll leave you alone.

Generally, you'll need to clean up the rice in the morning, and – if the nightly hauntings seem to continue – cast it again at night.

Though rice is the classic grain recommended in folklore, any small item can work, if there are enough of them.

Split peas, beans, and other objects can be used instead of rice. A bowl of salt next to your bed may work the same way. I've used coarse sea salt with success.

Tip: Be sure that everyone in the house knows what's on the floor, so there are no accidents if someone gets up for a midnight snack.

16

Religious Symbols - And a Warning

Some religious symbols seem to repel ghosts if you are spiritual – and perhaps even if you're not.

However, those symbols will be most effective if they reflect your own spirituality.

Most of this is easy and do-it-yourself (DIY), so I don't want to make it into something more mystical than it needs to be. However, there can be risks any time you delve into religious matters related to a haunting.

Obviously, if you're investigating someone *else's* home, their spirituality may not match yours. Even if you all attend the same church, temple, grove, or other community, don't assume their beliefs and practices are the same as yours. Tread cautiously.

In any home – including your own – you *might* be dealing with energy from past religious practices that may have lingering energy. At least 99% of the time, if religious energy lingers, it's good and beneficial.

Rarely, it's not. From my experience, those homes are few and far between. I hear rumors of them – possibly just urban legends – far more than I actually encounter them.

Religious symbols and haunted sites

You may recall an episode of "Haunted Collector," in which a *controversial* religious symbol was found underneath carpeting. It seemed to be part of the problem at that site.

That's not as unusual as it might seem.

Years ago, I investigated an extremely haunted New Hampshire home. It included a room with troubling symbols, similar to the "Haunted Collector" episode, and was altered in even more disturbing ways. (That house was going to be featured in the "Haunted Collector," but the homeowner backed out at the last minute. I've often wondered if the spirits influenced her decision. Either way, I never heard from her again.)

And, in almost every area where I've researched, I've seen homes in which – once the carpet was ripped up or a hidden closet exposed – they revealed something startling. Often, they were connected to covert – and troubling – spiritual practices.

Here's one important warning: If there is any possibility that you're dealing with something dark or demonic, don't use any religious symbols or rituals. They can make things worse instead of better.

Immediately, speak with an experienced demonologist (such as John Zaffis) or contact a community religious minister or advisor immediately.

(If you're not a religious person, that's okay. *Demons are a spiritual issue.* A spiritual professional – like a priest or minister – can refer you to someone who specializes in demonic and malicious entities. This is important: You don't need to share their spiritual beliefs.)

Some people regard demons – or demon-like activity – as aliens or from a different and dark time in Earth's history. Maybe they are, but that's not important. What matters is that they can be extremely dangerous.

However, demonic activity is very rare. In over 30 years of research, I've encountered something potentially demonic just a few times.

Take no chances. It's better to feel foolish when a minister assures you "it's nothing," or says it's just a misguided spirit, or even an angel – perhaps of a deceased family member – rather than a demon.

People often resolve troubling ghostly activity by putting faith-related symbols at windows and doors, or at least prominently displayed in the most haunted rooms.

So, if this is a normal (but annoying) haunting, you, too, may experience relief if you place religious symbols, statues, or artwork around your home.

Almost every religion has amulets or statues that repel evil spirits or ghosts. Christians often choose symbols of the Holy Spirit or St. Michael. I've also heard of non-Christians placing a Bible or crucifix in each room... and that worked. So, your personal beliefs may not matter as much as the ghost's.

If that doesn't work or you're not religious...

Sometimes (rarely), symbols from the homeowner's spirituality don't work. If that happens, use something that will impress the ghost.

That could be a religious symbol from their era and belief system. You may need to research the identity – or at least the time period – most likely to match your ghost.

See my tips about discovering your home's history. They're near the back of this book. (That field of research is called paragenealogy.)

Is yours a seasonal ghost?

- In the past, Puritans and some other faiths didn't approve of Christmas decorations.

- Until the 19th century, Christmas trees were generally regarded as Pagan.

- Halloween was a fearful night, also associated with misunderstood Pagan practices and beliefs.

- Easter eggs were linked with Pagan traditions as well and frowned upon by some faiths.

So, if your ghostly activity increases when you decorate for holidays, your ghost may be from a religious tradition that disapproves.

Either communicate your beliefs to your ghost, tell him (or her) not to be so overbearing, or ignore the ghost at those times of the year.

Remember that a ghost who reacts badly to Christmas isn't necessarily evil or demonic. Christmas celebrations were outlawed in England in the mid-17th century, and many Puritans in America were wholly intolerant of Christmas revels and decorations until around 1870, when the day became a Federal holiday.

If your ghost doesn't realize that time has passed, and beliefs and seasonal traditions have changed, you may have to be patient when the ghost seems disapproving or disruptive. After the holiday, things will return to normal.

17

Crystals for Neutralizing Energy

Many people find relief by placing crystals around their homes.

However, don't conclude that these are related to New Age or even Pagan beliefs.

For all we know, there may be some resonance between crystals' physical structure and ghosts' feelings about them. In the ghosts' realm, crystals may emit a sound or a smell that ghosts hate.

Frankly, we haven't a clue. Explaining how crystals work is like trying to prove that ghosts even exist. In other words, we're guessing.

We *do* have anecdotal evidence that some crystals provide relief at haunted sites.

Two ways to use crystals at haunted sites

You can choose crystals that ghosts don't seem to like, to repel them.

Or, you can use crystals that increase positive energy and empower you. Or, you can use both.

Some ghost hunters wear or carry hematite (or blood ore) to absorb negative energy. They believe that hematite can absorb troubling energy. Hematite has interesting magnetic properties, and – a bit of fun trivia: It's been identified on Mars. Some people think hematite's magnetic quality may repel ghosts, too.

It's also *possible* to resolve a haunting by placing a quartz crystal in each corner of the haunted room, or each corner of the home's basement. (I haven't tried it, but I've talked with several people who insist it's a nearly foolproof remedy.)

However, homes built on quartz report hauntings *more* often than those with no quartz nearby. So, if your haunted home is already on top of quartz, bringing more in may be a bad idea.

New Age stores can "prescribe" the correct crystals to help your home. You can also visit science and "rock hound" stores. Prices can vary widely.

When you purchase your crystals, ask the store owner to recommend the use and care of each.

Also, ask about cleansing your crystals. Some crystals must be removed (apparently taking the negative energy with them), cleansed or recharged, and then replaced.

Some people use sea salt or salt water to restore crystals' energy. Others believe that moonlight (from the full moon) is helpful.

I think these concepts – as explained – are highly speculative.

Nevertheless, some crystals seem to work in haunted settings. Hematite and quartz are often mentioned for repelling negative energy (including malicious and angry ghosts).

18

Mirrors and Dreamcatchers

Some homes are successfully protected by decorations. You may have seen those kinds of decorations in others' homes and not realized their purpose. Like crystals, we're not sure how or why they work, but centuries-old traditions say they do.

Two of the most popular are mirrors and dreamcatchers. According to folklore, both work best as protection, keeping ghosts out of a room or an entire house.

Note: You may have to banish the ghost first with a space-clearing technique mentioned in Chapters 11 and 12.

How to use dreamcatchers

There are two ways to use dreamcatchers. One is to hang them in the area where the ghostly energy seems the strongest.

The other is to hang one in every window and by every doorway in each haunted room.

That's all. Just display them in every space that might be an entrance to the haunted room.

Personally, I don't have much experience with this remedy, but at least – as decor – it can look nice. If it also prevents ghosts from entering the room or home, that's a plus.

Mirrors are a more controversial topic. I recommend using them with caution.

How to use mirrors

The most successful method is using a mirror to repel ghosts, keeping them outside the room – or entire residence – where they seem bothersome.

Place a mirror on your door – an exterior door (if the entire house seems haunted) or the door to the haunted room. The mirror should be facing *out* so – according to folklore – the ghost is startled when they look into it. In other words, the mirror is on the inside side of the door, attached so it faces towards the door. You won't see a reflection unless you have x-ray vision and can see through the door.

(Remember, people believe many ghosts can see through doors and walls. If the backward mirror might look odd to visitors, you can cover it with a poster or other decoration.)

However, keep a few other points in mind:

- Many believe that mirrors can be portals or passageways to another world. (Remember the "Erised" mirror in Harry Potter novels.)

- In my experience, at least half the time when someone complains about a haunted object, it's either a mirror or a doll/figure. (See my notes about haunted objects, near the back of this book.)

- I've seen images in mirrors at haunted sites... things that weren't in the room with us. It's almost always very creepy. Among the most notable were figures in reflections at Houmas House in Louisiana, and a historical home in the Haverhill, Massachusetts area.

- The "echoing" images in Maxmilian's diamond-backed mirrors at the Driskill Hotel in Austin, Texas, are eerie but very cool to see. If you're in the Austin area and a fan of haunted mirrors, they're worth a special visit.

- And then there are mirrors that – even when replaced – display hand prints and other images. The hallway mirror at the Myrtles Plantation is among them. (During one visit, I didn't see the handprint then, but it showed up in some of my photos... along with the reflection of a chandelier that wasn't in the room. Weird and fascinating!)

So, mirrors are supposed to be good to repel ghosts, *but mirrors may also be related to some hauntings.*

What to do with haunted mirrors

If a room is particularly haunted and contains a mirror, you may need to drape it with a dark cloth or remove it altogether.

(Personally, I'd take all mirrors out of the room, wrap each one – front and back – in opaque fabric, and store them in the tool shed or some location outside the home. Then, I'd see if anything changes in the room, or where the mirrors are stored, or both.)

In some cases, mirrors seem to reflect the image of the ghost. I've seen that at Houmas House in Louisiana and a Methuen, Massachusetts site. I also noted an odd reflection at Tudor World (aka The Falstaff Experience) in Stratford-upon-Avon, England, and at least one pub in York, England.

In my opinion, as long as the ghost remains an image in the mirror and it's merely startling to see it now and then, you don't need to do anything.

However, if it's worrisome, some people actually *collect* haunted objects. A local auction house or a site like eBay might not only get the mirror out of your home but also earn you a bit of profit.

19

Coping with a Scary Haunted House

There may be a fine line between angry ghosts and malicious spirits.

If safety is an issue, consult a professional. Don't hesitate. Get help.

As I've said before, don't try these techniques at home if the problem might be an evil entity or demon.

To be clear: If there is any possibility that the entity is malicious, *get out of your house* and *immediately* contact a local member of the religious community.

Nuisance ghosts

If you're dealing with an annoying, belligerent ghost, the following methods may help.

Some ghosts don't like garlic cloves or bowls of salt. Put one next to your bed. (According to readers' reports, a bowl of salt by the bed seems to work best.)

According to legend – and many ghost hunters' reports – ghosts don't like to cross a line of salt. Place a line of salt across your doorways, or even around your house. (But first, be sure that the ghosts have left the house.)

Sea salt may be best, and many people use *blessed* sea salt. (Many people routinely bless the food before the meal. Blessing salt doesn't have to be any different, though you could ask a priest or minister to bless it for extra spiritual energy to repel evil.)

This is worth repeating: *Be sure that the ghost is out of the room (or the entire house) before you complete the line of salt.*

Otherwise, you might trap the spirit in the house; if folklore is correct, the ghost won't cross the line of salt to get *out.*

Holy water is another tried-and-true remedy for hauntings. You do not have to be religious to use it, but it's better if you are.

Note: Under no circumstances use holy water if you might be dealing with a demon. The term "demon" refers to a specific kind of entity or energy, and it is so dangerous that I cannot recommend trying to banish it yourself. Speak with a trusted member of your community's religiosity. If they aren't authorized and trained to deal with demons, ask them to refer you to someone who is.

(Note: That is entirely different from the religious concept of *possession* by demons. Various Christian faiths delve into that topic in depth, from the Old Testament Book of Samuel, to the Book of Enoch, and so on. That is a different topic altogether.)

Online, you'll find a variety of rituals to enhance the effects of holy water in your home.

Or, you can ask a priest or minister to bless your house. That may be the best – and safest – choice.

20

Special Situations - Children and Teens

Different approaches may be necessary when a family with children or teens is troubled by ghosts.

Children and pets seem more sensitive to ghosts and spirits than adults. Teenagers can bring their own energy to the mix and even attract unwelcome spirits.

The following advice is for families dealing with a benign ghost or a situation in which a child believes they have a ghost but doesn't have one.

Help for children

A movie like "Casper" may calm a frightened child if the haunting is mild and not dangerous.

Movies like "The Canterbury Ghost" may be charming but might encourage a child's involvement with an unseen entity. That's rarely a good idea. Save that movie for older children and young teens.

Your public library may recommend other "happy" ghost stories.

However, consult professionals immediately if your children could be traumatized by what's going on in your home – whether or not it's an actual ghost. Remember that ghosts are spirits, so your best choice may be a *spiritual* advisor. Start with your religious leader, such as a priest or minister.

A few paranormal researchers specialize in helping families with children cope with ghosts.

Help for teens

Teens may enjoy "Ghostbusters" and similar movies. Those movies include frightening images and concepts, but plenty that's ridiculous, too. Teens who see role models in the "Ghostbuster" heroes, might also be empowered by them.

Poltergeists

If you are dealing with a poltergeist (literally, a "noisy ghost") that's causing mischief, the activity may be *related* to a teen in your home, or anyone else on an emotional (or hormonal) roller coaster.

It's a murky topic in some ways. You can learn more about poltergeists and emotional ghosts near the back of this book.

The more baffling, worrisome, and persistent the haunting, the more critical it is to consult a professional. My best advice is to talk with a trusted member of your *local* religious community, *not someone you've found online.*

Even after many years in this field, if something frightened me in my home, I'd find someone who knows more about spirits and entities than I do.

The subject is far too broad for anyone to "know it all." I may be an expert at predicting where hauntings will be reported. I may also be one of the best in the field for understanding patterns of hauntings – geographic, time-specific, and so on.

However, I'm an amateur when it comes to *dangerous* entities. I know what *isn't* a ghost... but I can't always be sure what else it might be, and especially what to do about it if it's malicious, territorial, or aggressive.

Never take a chance when safety is an issue.

If your "gut feeling" tells you you're in danger, take that internal warning seriously. We have no proof of *anything* paranormal. We can make educated guesses, but they're still guesses.

Above all, never put your children at risk. They may be far more vulnerable than you realize.

21

Professional Resources

If you've tried everything in this book and nothing has worked, it may be time to seek outside help – more than just a home inspector or local amateur ghost hunter.

Ask your friends and family if they know anyone who's lived in a haunted house. (You can make this sound like a normal question, and lead into it by mentioning a recent TV show about ghosts.)

You might discover that your home is well-known as a "haunted" house, and everyone assumes you already know about it. You could also learn that your family has a hereditary ghost or two. This spirit may be a protector, such as a benevolent ancestor or a Banshee. (Banshees do *not* cause death or tragedy. In fact, they protect families, usually those with Irish ancestry.)

This kind of information can transform a frightening experience into something less scary.

If you belong to a church, ask your spiritual leaders for advice. They've probably dealt with ghost questions in the past. At this level, help should be free or very inexpensive... no more than the price of lunch in a nice restaurant. Remember, you're dealing with a *spirit*. Your first line of defense and protection will probably be spiritual.

Even if you don't believe in God or go to church, a local priest or minister may be your best resource when dealing with a ghost.

Also remember: Bad advice can be worse than doing nothing. If you're not wholly comfortable with the advice you receive, keep looking.

The time to get a second opinion is *before* anyone comes into your home and stirs up the energy.

Always ask:

• What do you plan to do? (Get specifics: What they'll do, when and how often they'll visit, and what they do to follow up.)

• What are the risks? (If the person says "none," run the other way.)
• How much experience have you had, in this kind of work?
• Do I know anyone this has worked for? (Check that reference.)
• If this doesn't work, what's next? (Get a firm commitment.)
• What will this cost? (Almost all priests and ministers advise people free of charge.)

If local resources aren't able to help you, or the problem is severe, you may need to look for more professional help... the next level among spiritual and paranormal practitioners.

When you *must* seek professional help

1. Is the haunting creating health or safety issues? That includes breathing difficulties, disorientation on stairways, or poltergeist activity involving bruising, broken objects, or fire hazards. If your answer is yes, get professional help now.

2. Have you tried many remedies, but nothing else helped, so far? Are you or your family members exhausted from anxiety? If you're losing sleep, or if family members are so stressed, they're snapping at each other, get help now.

Of course, if anyone in your family is taking medications or self-medicating with alcohol specifically because of ghost-related issues, this problem can't wait. Call someone right now.

This may sound repetitive, but even if you feel embarrassed, or overwhelmed by persistent "weird" problems in your home: You *must* consult a professional if ghost-like activity is impacting your life or jeopardizing your well-being.

Two kinds of professionals can provide the best help: Experienced spiritual advisors (especially those trusted by their churches for matters that might be demonic), and respected paranormal investigators. No matter which you choose, they should have extensive experience with ghosts and hauntings, and provide references that you can check.

Religious options

If you might be dealing with a demon or a dangerous entity, don't take chances. Spiritual options for haunted houses include everything from having your house blessed, to a full exorcism. Your local priest, minister, or other spiritual leader can recommend resources. Even if you don't consider yourself a religious person, visit a church in your town. It won't be as awkward as you might think.

If you're skeptical of religions

If you're strongly opposed to getting help from the religious community, seek experienced, respected paranormal investigators.

• Ask for references, and check them. That's your number one protection from scammers and inept teams that actually make things worse.

• Ask how long they've worked in this field. Look for proof. Being "interested in ghosts since childhood" doesn't count.

• If they have a website, see how professional it looks and how long it's been online. (Use a free "WhoIs" lookup site to check the history of their domain name.)

• Check YouTube for their videos. (TikTok isn't enough.) Many researchers and teams have channels. You'll learn a lot about their professionalism, skills, and attitudes from those videos. If their videos are all "jump scares" and rely almost entirely on customized radios and AI devices, they're probably not a good resource.

• Remember that almost anyone can have a website, radio show, or TV show. (I've turned down dozens of TV producers over the past 20+ years.) Some TV "stars" have *no* real experience and *no idea* what they're doing. They were cast because producers thought they'd appeal to the viewing audience... period. In the real world of ghost hunting, experience, skill, and happy clients are all that matter.

• Ask the police and Better Business Bureau if anyone has complained.

Questions to ask

• How soon can you begin? (You need help *now.)*

• Exactly what will you do? (Get details about tools and techniques. If occult tools such as a Ouija board might be involved, say no, and end the conversation.)

• How long have your team members been with you? (Anything under six months is a big red flag.)

• Do you carry liability insurance? Are your team members bonded, and for what risks?

• How much time will you need? (Get specific dates and hours.)

• If my house is haunted, what will you do to help? (Get details and a commitment.)

Get everything in writing, especially when they'll be in your home, how long they'll stay, and what they'll do in terms of a follow-up.

Note: There are no "ghost hunting licenses." Be very skeptical if someone claims to be licensed as a paranormal investigator. Likewise, a "certified" paranormal researcher has only earned a certificate from some course. (In the past, I offered a free, online ghost hunting course. In the final lesson, I'd included a certificate of completion, but it wasn't professional or an endorsement. I removed it when I saw people downloading the certificate without going through the lessons.)

Most paranormal investigators do not charge clients for this kind of work. They may ask you to cover their reasonable travel expenses, but that's all.

The vast majority of ghost hunters are good, sincere people. However, you're particularly vulnerable when a ghost frightens you and your family. It's better to be too skeptical than too trusting.

If you need professional help with your haunted house, be sure you know (a) who's entering your home, and (b) that they're the best possible people to help you.

Just because the team is willing to work for free... that doesn't mean you have to settle for amateurs.

When help arrives

When you ask for help, and the person or team arrives at your home, if you aren't comfortable with them, speak up immediately.

• If they do anything that troubles you, say so.

• If they seem to be provoking the ghost/s or making things worse, ask the team leader to explain what's going on. Don't accept double-talk meant to impress you. Get well-grounded answers that you're comfortable with.

• If anyone appears to be on drugs, or has alcohol on his/her breath, tell him or her to leave. No exceptions. If others object, ask them all to leave.

• If someone is belligerent or doesn't leave when asked, call the police immediately. Don't try to negotiate with someone who tries to intimidate you, especially using fear tactics related to ghosts and paranormal entities. A bully is a bully, no matter what the context.

• If anyone is dogmatic about their answers, or has a "my way or the highway" attitude, turn them out. Most paranormal researchers are either deeply spiritual and sympathetic to ghost-related problems, or they're by-the-numbers clinical about this research. We're frank about things we don't have answers for... yet. A "know it all" in this field is usually green enough to be a danger to himself and others, in haunted settings.

You don't need an excuse to ask people to leave.

Your safety and your family's may depend on your judgment. It's better to seem rude, paranoid, or weird than to take chances.

If the team won't allow you to remain in your home during the investigation, find out why. If you have any reason to be concerned, you may want to continue looking for an investigator or team you trust more. Or, lock up your valuables and place webcams around the house so you can review their work later.

In the early 21st century, these kinds of precautions never crossed our minds. Today, things are very different.

We don't know everything about ghosts. Nobody does. In fact, much of what's said about ghosts is pure speculation. There is never just one answer to issues related to hauntings.

If you're not happy with the results of any investigation, call some-one else or return to your priest or minister for further suggestions.

When all else fails, remember that ghosts (and entities that can seem like ghosts) are spirits. Spiritual counselors – religious people – usually have a broader understanding of spirits than people who gleaned their expertise from TV shows and a few amateur investigations.

As I've said, you don't have to believe in the religion of the person helping you. It's not the context, but the education and experiences of the minister (or priest, or imam, or rabbi, etc.) that may provide answers when nothing else seems to.

22

Crossing Over

Some people believe they can help spirits "cross over" to the afterlife.

That may be possible. I've heard many stories – conveyed sincerely – in which the person spoke of simply telling the ghost to "go to the light," or something similar. And then – with a sense of relief – the ghost left the site, happily and permanently.

I've never witnessed that happening. Not at a site that I could revisit to see if anything had genuinely changed.

I don't want to discount that. It's possible – perhaps even logical – that it happens, now and then.

Personally, I find it more reassuring to seek the assistance of a local priest, minister, or other spiritual professional when dealing with a *problematic* ghostly entity.

If you've tried everything I've said so far, and you're confident that your home is haunted and you cannot live with it, you need additional help.

This is especially true if the ghost seems extremely emotional, either persistently angry or deeply anguished. (Frankly, most ghosts don't seem that interested in communicating with the living.)

I've heard stories of sympathetic people dropping their personal boundaries, assuring the "ghost" that friends and family awaited them on "the other side," and so on... But then, the entity turned vicious, and the person felt personally and spiritually attacked.

In my view, the potential risks of dealing with hostile spirits are significant. While it's *possible* that you're dealing with a confused or fearful ghost, there's also the chance that you're facing a cunning and malevolent entity, such as a demon or malicious spirit.

My advice should be clear: Do *not* take chances. If you find a ghostly entity in your home and there is *any* possibility that it is malicious, it's crucial to contact a respected member of your local religious community for help.

Or, if you encounter a lost or fearful ghost at a haunted site outside your home, tell a local religious minister. Then, it's up to them to decide the best way to help the ghostly entity.

23

Conclusion

The vast majority of "haunted" homes aren't haunted at all.

Even those with paranormal activity – the ghostly kind – usually don't have ghosts. It's just odd activity we can only explain in paranormal terms (outside everyday phenomena).

And, only a very tiny percentage of homes with entities have spirits worth worrying about.

More significant dangers include carbon monoxide poisoning, sustained and high EMF levels, and floors or staircases that could cause accidents or injuries.

It's essential to take seriously every report of a haunted house. Even if it's your home and you feel silly making a big deal about it... do so, anyway.

Something is worrying you. It's important to find out what it is.

You'll usually find a normal (if unusual) explanation. It's often something simple to repair.

Remember, none of us have absolute proof of ghosts. We might believe in them, but we can't prove anything.

Everything we say (including what's in this book) is speculation. It may be based on decades of trial-and-error testing, but it's still speculation.

Frankly, anyone who claims otherwise is dangerous. They may put others in harm's way, too.

I can't imagine anything worse than an investigator or team telling a client that a house is haunted... but it was carbon monoxide or elevated EMF that led to illness (or worse).

Of course, your problem could be two-pronged: Your house needs repairs *and* has paranormal activity.

Start with an open mind. First, explore the normal (if odd) answers and explanations. While doing so, rule out real-life dangers.

There's nothing woo-woo or weird in that, and it's where every ghost hunter and paranormal investigator must start.

Above all, don't think your concerns are silly. Get answers. Find out what's *really* going on in your home or your client's.

Lives may depend on it, not because ghosts are especially dangerous (they're not) but because the real explanation may be something normal, putting you at risk.

If something in your home is bothering you, get an answer now.

24

Appendix

The most important information is at the front of this book.

- From my experience, about 80% of "haunted" houses aren't haunted. Many ghost-like issues are the result of something normal. Often, those can be resolved with basic home repairs.

- If your home really *is* haunted, most cases are residual energy hauntings. You're in no danger, and you can make minor changes to be less troubled by your haunted house.

- In general, even the most haunted home can be resolved with the help of a member of your local mainstream religious community.

The first part of this book provides diagnostics. I hope they helped you discover what's going on and whether it's actually paranormal.

If you're still not sure, combined insights by a home inspector and an experienced paranormal investigator can give you a good second (and third) opinion, based on anomalous activity.

Weigh your options carefully. Then, choose what to do.

If you or anyone in your household feels at risk, everyone should leave the home immediately and help. What you're dealing with might be a benign haunting, but it might not. Take no chances.

The following sections can give you additional information.

25

What Not to Do

Only a few things can cause more problems than you had when you started looking for answers.

The biggest danger is waiting and hoping things will improve on their own.

Usually, they won't.

If you're reading this book because you think your house might be haunted, keep a detailed journal of what's happening – immediately.

You might be pleasantly surprised to see how little is actually going on or how easily it can be explained (and repaired) once you examine the bigger picture.

Or, you might realize that the problem is bigger and more constant than you'd imagined. In that case, *don't wait for things to get worse.* Do something about this today.

Here are some other warnings:

1. If you feel in danger, even if you think it sounds foolish, get out of the house and call someone immediately. For many people, it's easiest to call a friend who has dealt with ghosts, or a member of your local religious community (a priest, minister, etc.). If you can't think of anyone else, call the police.

2. If you feel you're even mildly at risk, don't try *any* steps in this book (even the "Easy - DIY" ones) by yourself. If you're already working with a professional and you're still frightened or aren't sure the person is doing their job, get a second opinion right away.

3. Do not use anything occult, such as a Ouija board, and do not allow those items in your home. Ghosts are not performers, and some Ouija or "spirit board" experiments have gone terribly wrong.

If you've already caused problems with a Ouija board, do not burn it; some people say the ashes can spread related, dangerous energy. Bury it at least a foot deep, usually at the foot of a tree. (I'm not sure why this works, but several people have recommended it.)

You can also dispose of haunted and occult objects at a landfill site, as long as they are buried, not burned, and not recovered by scavengers.

I also advise against bringing in a channel medium. A channel medium is someone who, in a trance state, allows the ghost or spirit entity to speak "through" the medium's body. In a dangerous haunted setting, this can empower any malicious entities and put the medium at risk as well.

4. Even if everything seemed fine at the start, get out of the house immediately if you become frightened at any point in this process. That's equally true if a family member (especially a child) feels threatened by ghost-related activity. Stay with friends, family, a hotel, a motel, or even a shelter until all of the problems are resolved. (I'll say that repeatedly. Too much is at risk. Often, people don't take adequate precautions, thinking they'll look silly, fleeing from something that friends or family may feel is "all in their imagination.")

5. Do not use holy water unless you are certain that it's a ghost, not a malicious spirit or demon.

If you're not sure, consult an experienced, respected demonologist such as John Zaffis. Demons and evil entities are rare despite what you see on TV and in movies. However, don't take a chance if you're dealing with an extreme haunting.

6. If the problem returns, don't assume the previous efforts didn't work. Some repairs may need to be revisited. Also, especially with intense hauntings, repeating the reduction or banishing steps may be necessary. Try again.

Once again: Do not stay anywhere that you don't feel safe.

If you are anxious about what's going on, get the help that you need immediately. This includes medical, spiritual, emotional, and mental health counseling when appropriate.

26

More Historical Resources

As any family history librarian will tell you, there is a wealth of records to help you understand who lived in your house... and who may haunt it.

First, find out who lived in your home in the past. Talk with them or research those who have passed.

Probate records may be one of the best resources – usually searched by professional genealogists.

Wills often record each person's true feelings. They know the will won't be read until after the person's death, so the will is where the person vents. I've seen bequests like, "To my niece, Hilda, who always had to add her two cents to conversations, I leave two cents." (In that case, it wouldn't surprise me if Hilda was haunted by the aunt or uncle, too.)

If you conduct probate research yourself, check property disputes and other court records while you're at the courthouse.

For example, you may discover a running argument between two neighbors. Both may be haunting – and maintaining their claims – after death.

Peace of mind

Once you know who your ghost is, and whether or not the ghost is upset or "just visiting," you'll probably feel more comfortable in your haunted home.

Remember: We have evidence that some "ghosts" are alive in their own worlds, parallel to ours. In that case, there's nothing to banish, although significantly redecorating your home might help, so there's less resonance with the parallel realm.

Also, I've heard – from wholly trusted researchers – that some *apparent* ghosts perceive us in *their* worlds, and they think *we're* the ghosts.

Knowing this information can put your mind at rest and enable you to live in harmony with your ghosts.

<h1 style="text-align:center">27</h1>

Weather, Seasonal Changes, and Events

Weather and changing seasons can explain many odd and startling phenomena. For example, animals can behave strangely shortly before a storm arrives. They're not constantly reacting to ghosts.

Some people are sensitive to barometric changes, too. They'll complain of unexplained aches and pains, or feel worried or sad. When the storm breaks, they feel relief.

Dry heat and damp weather

Your house and floorboards may creak dramatically for days, weeks, or even a month after you first turn on the heat for the winter. Doors, no longer swollen tight in their frames, can seem to open or close on their own. They'll rattle more when the wind blows, too.

Likewise, when humid weather returns, floorboards can creak again. Doors suddenly seem to resist you, or – with the added weight of the moisture wood absorbs – they suddenly start swinging open, or close on their own.

As humidity increases, your basement, kitchen, and bathrooms may acquire mold and mildew in rarely seen areas. You can feel uncomfortable in those areas if you're sensitive to mold and mildew. Then, *looking for a reason,* you (or a client) might worry that it's a ghost. (This issue isn't just seasonal. If you use a humidifier, vaporizer, or dehumidifier, they can affect sounds and smells around your home, too.)old weather issues

Ice can work its way into your roof or the exterior or foundation of your home. As it expands and contracts, strange noises can result. Most people describe them as creaking or moaning.

Basement walls can produce odd noises as the ground next to them freezes. People sometimes describe those noises as teeth grinding or a demonic growl. Basement stairs can swell with humidity, or shrink when a furnace dries them out. Walking on those stairs can seem different or even disorienting compared to what you're used to.

Check with your neighbors. Ask if they're having similar issues in their homes. If it's a seasonal issue and your neighbor's home is similar to yours, they may have the same issues.

Wood stoves, barbecues, and fireplaces

If you or a neighbor has a wood stove or fireplace, the particulate in the smoke can trigger allergies, headaches, and sometimes disorientation.

If someone uses a barbecue, the lighter fluid or heat source (gas, coal, wood, or trash) can also present issues with some people.

Rarely, I have seen people become irritable for no apparent reason, until they discovered that an unexpected source had triggered an allergy.

It's rarely enough to make someone think his home is haunted, but – combined with other odd events – it could be a contributing factor.

Seasonal Affected Disorder (SAD)

When people move from a sunny climate to an area where clouds are normal, they may not realize the impact of the change. Depression can result. In turn, that can lead to various issues that can seem like a haunting or even demonic influences.

An unusually cloudy autumn, winter, or spring can have the same effect, no matter where you live.

Moving to a house with more north-facing windows can also trigger a SAD effect. If you (or your clients) have just moved into the home, check the windows and recent weather conditions. Sunny weather or treatments for SAD might be all that's needed.

Climate issues

Climates have changed slightly in recent years. A few degrees difference – higher or lower – can dramatically change how a house responds.

We've seen record-breaking heat and cold in some areas. Water tables have risen in some regions, increasing humidity and affecting the foundations of houses.

So, though your house (or your client's) never made these noises before, temperature and humidity changes might explain them now.

Recent weather changes must always be considered when evaluating a site if the ghost reports (or concerns) also developed recently.

Holidays

Christmas trees (or sprays used on them) can trigger allergies that make you feel something's wrong, and maybe your home is haunted.

But, the holidays are fraught with *other* issues if a home already has a ghost, even if he (or she) usually keeps a low profile.

Christmas trees can offend some ghosts. The tree, the star on the top, and – to the ghost – commercialism (even without dogs barking Christmas carols) push the ghost too far.

Halloween is supposed to be the most haunted night of the year. Traditionally, that's a day (and night) when the veil is thinnest. It's also a "Pagan" celebration that can offend some Christian spirits, so they're more active at that time of year. (That's always seemed like a "Catch 22" to me.)

At the other end of the calendar, the last night of April (Walpurgis and other celebrations) can be nearly as haunted as Halloween. Expect more actual ghostly activity then, too.

Easter is another festival that can offend some Christian spirits and others. The "veil" may not be thinner then, but never underestimate the wrath of the ghost of a 17th-century Puritan minister who objects to Easter eggs and Easter bunnies.

Costumed events

If a living history event is nearby – people in costumes, replicating events from the past – it's not unusual to hear reports of ghosts wandering nearby. Whether they're actual ghosts or just residual energy stirred up by the resonance of the events... well, that's anyone's guess. Just keep it in mind if ghost complaints seem to pop up "out of nowhere," around the time of an historic re-enactment or celebration.

28

Hot and Cold Spots

Haunted houses are famous for having "cold spots." (Hot spots are rare, but they do occur and can be more worrisome.)

Those are defined areas where the temperature seems more than five degrees higher or lower than the space around it. (I prefer to limit my research to changes of 15 degrees F, or more.) You can usually feel the temperature drop by holding your hands in the cold spot. (Hot spots are generally described as a blast of hot air on the face or a general, full-body sense of entering a hot area.)

If you're not sure what a cold spot feels like, there's probably one at a haunted site near you.

Some famous "cold spots"

- One notable cold spot is above the Joseph W. Gilson gravestone at Gilson Road Cemetery, Nashua, NH. For about 15 years, I could rely on when training team members, to show what a cold spot feels like. However, during later research trips, that cold spot was elusive and unreliable. So, things can change, even at reliable haunts.

- Another well-known cold spot is at the fireplace in the Red Room, upstairs at Brennan's restaurant in New Orleans' French Quarter. You can feel it directly in front of the mantle, and about six inches below it.

- The Myrtles Plantation main building has multiple cold spots. (Check to be sure you're not in the path of an air conditioning vent.) I've experienced bone-chilling cold temperatures upstairs in the main bedroom, even with the a/c turned off.

- Cold spots move around the Tudor World site in Stratford-upon-Avon, England. (That's one of the most extraordinary and profoundly haunted places I've ever investigated.)

- You'll also find cold spots in the famous Tower of London and in the basement at Warwick Castle.

- Mt. Auburn Cemetery in Cambridge, Massachusetts, has many graves with cold spots over or near them. That's not a huge surprise since it's a "country club cemetery" (with the tombs of many wealthy and influential people). Some ghost hunters joke, "Powerful *in* life, and powerful *after,* as well." I agree.

Hot spots, too?

Some of the best first-person "hot spot" stories were told to me by a retired New Hampshire police chief. He indicated several locations – in confidence – that no one has mentioned in connection with investigations.

The retired police chief seemed to think the heat was from something malicious. That's a big red flag warning me to stay away.

I'm comfortable with cold spots. They're well-defined and often in interesting locations.

In paranormal studies, some people believe that cold represents an area where the ghost might be drawing energy. However, there is no evidence that a cold spot indicates anything evil.

Likewise, misty breath does not indicate that a ghost is nearby. That only happens in the movies... or if someone's playing a prank.

Is it REALLY cold?

Measure the cold spot.

The biggest mistake is using a point-and-shoot device – a digital, remote thermometer – that measures the temperature of objects, not the air. Be sure that your thermometer measures ambient air temperature.

If it's significantly (at least five to ten degrees) higher or lower than the area around it, look for normal explanations. Generally, the movement of a candle flame will indicate a draft from outside or from the a/c. In hot spots, remember that heat rises. So, the air movement may be more vertical than horizontal. A fluffy feather duster is ideal for detecting drafts in multiple directions.

If there's no *reasonable* explanation why one small area (usually just a couple of feet in diameter, or less) is cold or hot, it *can* suggest a haunting.

Check with a home heating expert before jumping to conclusions. A weird gap in insulation or an unexpected leak from a heating or cooling vent could be the simple answer.

29

Poltergeists

Poltergeists are an enigma. The term usually refers to unexplained noises or moving objects, ghostly slaps, and similar prankish activity often attributed to a ghost.

> Trivia: The word "poltergeist" originated in the German language, and is composed of the verb "polter," meaning "to make a noise," and the noun "geist," meaning "ghost." The concept has a long history. Martin Luther (1483 – 1546) used the term in his writings. The first English use of that word may have been in Catherine Crowe's 1850 book of ghost stories, in which she described a mischievous spirit as "what the Germans call the *poltergeist,* or racketing spectre."

Poltergeists are annoying but rarely demonic. However, this subject is *very* controversial. We don't have enough evidence and cases can vary widely.

Many professionals believe the problems are created by someone (not a ghost) in the vicinity using psychokinesis, a form of ESP that enables them to create and manipulate physical phenomena.

Others think a ghost *may* be involved, drawing energy from anyone on an emotional or hormonal roller coaster. Usually – but not always – that's a teenager. (What the ghost does with that energy... that's unpredictable, and can include *turning the energy on its source*.)

The effects seem to continue even when the energy source (such as the teen) is five miles away.

So far, we've seen the best results when the emotional person (the energy source) receives counseling.

However, even without counseling, the problem will usually go away on its own, in weeks or months.

Is water involved?

We've noticed a direct relationship between the presence of water (sometimes unexplained) and poltergeist activity. Colin Wilson was among the first researchers to notice this.

People report more poltergeist activity around kitchens.

At the other extreme: If there's *no* water in the area, small puddles – about the size of coins – can appear once that particular poltergeist session concludes. Look for it. (I'm not sure if anyone's run tests to determine the composition of that residual water.)

Safety first!

If poltergeist activity occurs, keep sharp objects in cabinets or drawers. This is especially true in rooms with water, such as kitchens, bathrooms, darkrooms, and any room with a fish tank.

Remember, there is no evidence of a ghost killing anyone, ever. (In tales such as the Bell Witch story, there's significant evidence that injuries were caused by a *living* person, not a ghost.)

However, poltergeists can cause injuries, and they're especially worrisome around stairs and heat sources.

If poltergeist activity is an issue, speak with a professional about it.

30

Orbs and Other Ghost Photos

Orbs don't always indicate ghostly activity. Never *start* with an orb photo and *then* go looking for ghosts. Anomalies like ghost photos are – at best – only *supporting* evidence.

People send me photos of orbs, strange misty figures, double exposures, or deliberately created images daily.

They ask if that's a ghost.

An experienced photographer can usually recognize an orb that's an anomaly instead of one caused by moisture, insects, dust, and reflections.

I tell people to save the first 100 (or more) "orb" photos they take. *Then,* go back and study them closely. You may be able to spot the difference between false orbs and those we can't explain.

Ghost photos are only as reliable as the expertise and integrity of the photographer.

Orb photos

Is there an orb in your photos? Here's how to spot fake and not-ghostly orbs:

- The number one culprit is exhaling while you're taking a flash photo. Even on warm, humid nights, your breath can add enough moisture to create orbs and other anomalies. The solution is to hold your breath immediately before and when you take each photo. Also, take two photos quickly; a false orb's appearance will change, or might be in one photo and not the next.

- Dust and pollen can create perfectly circular orbs, but they're often somewhat dotted or have visible flecks near the center of the orb.

• Insects usually form irregular-shaped orbs, or may leave an irregular trail of light behind them.

• Reflections – especially reflections of the flash on your camera – usually look like classic (if muted) lens flares. Search for "lens flares" online. You'll see photos with telltale lines – often star-like – extending from the center of the orb or light source. Others form a halo around the central light source or reflection.

• Rain and snow usually create blurry and too-solid orbs. On a damp night, you may see hundreds of overlapping orbs in a photo. (You can replicate this by taking pictures with mist from a spray bottle filled with water.)

• Orbs in basement photos are usually the result of humidity; there are too many of them. Orbs in attics are generally bits of dust stirred up as people move around the room. A flashlight – normal or UV – can help reveal those particles, especially as they're stirred up by people walking around the room.

• Indoors, see if the picture was taken near an air freshener that sprays a mist regularly. That's unusual, but I've seen a few impressive examples.

Are orbs proof?

An orb photo may *support* other ghostly evidence, but – on its own – an orb photo isn't proof of paranormal activity. Don't let anyone frighten you by showing a photo – especially a photo of you or someone close to you – with an orb nearby.

While the orb *may* be Great-Aunt Agnes saying "hello" in the photo, it's *not* hard evidence of a ghost or anything else paranormal.

Test your cameras with dust, pollen, moisture, and reflections, to see what those orbs look like. (No two cameras are likely to photograph false orbs exactly alike. Know what your false orb "fingerprints" look like.)

Anomalous orbs in haunted settings are – by definition – orbs that don't look like anything you can explain in normal terms.

Remember, even a convincing "ghost photo" (or even a series of photos) *doesn't mean you have a ghost.* It might support other evidence, but – in the absence of many other anomalies – ghost photos don't *prove* anything. They're fun. They're intriguing. However, please don't take them seriously... not unless it's comforting to think that orb in the wedding photo is the spirit of your favorite Aunt Clementine.

Indoor orbs are common. Before flat-screen computer monitors became popular, I'd receive three to five computer-related orb photos daily. People worried that they had a haunted computer. Each had no other reasons to suspect a haunting, just a photo showing something orb-like near their computer. (I'm not kidding.)

Any shiny surface – including glass, metal, polished wood, or mirrors – can reflect the flash of a camera and create orbs in a photograph. They're usually refracted light. Once you know what you're looking for, they can be very easy to spot.

Ghostly mist

Smoke is rarely a problem in photos, even if the smoker is beside the camera. That surprised me. I'd attributed many photos of misty shapes and apparitions to smoke.

Pipe smoke is a little more problematic, but not a huge issue. Besides, you'll likely notice the fragrance if smoke lands nearby. Incense is the only reliable source of eerie smoke images, and even they are easy to identify. Smoke from incense is very dense and usually reflects the flash as vivid white or pale blue lines, usually wavy lines.

Misty areas in outdoor photos can be early evidence of fog arriving, not ghosts. However, fog and moisture aren't as problematic as I once thought.

So, in my experience, the only consistently baffling "ghost photos" occur when the photographer exhales while taking the photo.

Ghost research (and author) Sean Paradis was the first to mention this to me as a significant problem, during a Tenney Gate House investigation in Methuen, Massachusetts (USA). We were photographing ruins near the top of the hill, and his breath created some startling images.

We tried a few tests and confirmed that it was just his breath. That led me to about two years of breath experiments in various climates, weather conditions, and light conditions. (When I test theories, I try to be very thorough.)

Hair and camera straps

Even a single hair in front of the camera can look eerie. On a dark night, you may see a spiral, slightly textured shape highlighted by your camera's flash. It's easy to see why people think they're vortices.

Camera straps can be another overlooked issue. Initially, that was confusing, as – in most cases – at least one end of the camera strap seems to "vanish."

(During my early ghost research using cameras, I thought both ends of the camera strap would always appear in the photo. I was wrong.)

Depending on how the camera strap catches the light, both ends can seem to vanish, leaving a weird, textured, worm-like shape in your photo.

Test effects like these with your own camera.

Once you know, you know

I dedicated nearly six years to studying orbs in photos. Before those tests, I thought most orbs – even the most convincing photos – were probably dust, bugs, moisture, or reflections.

I was wrong. It's very difficult to create convincing-looking orbs with dust, moisture, etc.

Of course, even if an orb or other anomaly *looks* convincing, you'll still want to look for normal explanations. However, from my experience, dust, rain, humidity, and bugs rarely cause convincing-looking orbs.

My best advice is: Don't exhale while taking a photo in a possibly haunted site. Resulting orbs and filmy white shapes are difficult to evaluate. Even I can't always tell the difference between an exhale and a legitimate anomaly.

31

Provoking

Provoking means antagonizing a spirit so it responds and its activity can be observed.

One or more investigators will shout at, challenge, tease, or taunt the ghost to evoke a response. The language can be abusive and almost always harsh.

Provoking is a practice of last resort. **I never use it.**

However, I realize that provoking *can* be necessary in some situations. For example, an investigating team might find *no* evidence of paranormal activity. Provoking may be the *only practical way* to determine if a house is or isn't haunted. Not unless the team can return several times.

(One of my team members is jokingly called "ghost bait." If he's with me, ghosts will usually make themselves known. Every ghost hunting team should have someone like him, if possible. But, admittedly, people like him are rare.)

Provoking should never be used in a situation unless it's absolutely necessary. Taunting or challenging a spirit is mean, cruel, and dangerous.

Ghosts aren't here to entertain us. (One exception might be theatre ghosts, but they rarely need encouragement – or provoking – to manifest.)

It's inconsiderate to taunt ghosts, leaving the homeowner to deal with the angry spirits. Unfortunately, it happens far too often with amateur investigators. They've seen provoking on TV, and they think "everyone does it." (No, we don't.)

If a team member unexpectedly provokes a ghost in your home, stop the investigation immediately. Ensure that the team tells you what they'll do to resolve the problem before leaving your home.

An angry, agitated ghost is a liability you – and the team – cannot afford.

What to do after provocation

Sometimes, people unintentionally provoke a ghost.

You're not the problem... it's the *ghost.* The spirit may not like *anyone* – you or a professional helping you – investigating "his" home. Or, a ghost may feel that a particular room is "hers." (I saw that at the haunted carriage house at the Spalding Inn, in Whitefield, New Hampshire.)

Sometimes, it's best to leave the ghost alone as much as possible. In time, they may get used to you being there.

You don't have to be *obsessively* cautious, just don't get them riled. Treat them like you would any other roommate. Ask visitors to your home (including ghost investigators) to do the same.

After provoking – intentional or accidental – resolutions vary.

Sometimes, an apology is necessary. The apology might have to be profuse to the point of silliness. Some ghosts are very sensitive.

Or, the provoker may need to promise never to return... *and then stay away.*

It's a case-by-case issue. Patience – and lots of it – may be necessary, while the investigator finds something to resolve the problem.

If the issue is extreme, you and your family could leave and stay with friends, family, or at a local hotel for three days. In most cases, annoying ghostly energy – activity churned up by an investigation – will stop within 72 hours.

Are YOU being provoked?

As I mentioned earlier, evidence suggests that some ghosts aren't spirits of the deceased. They're living people, in a parallel world or dimension. They just happen to perceive us (and think we're ghosts), or vice versa.

It's possible that what you *think* is an angry ghost or a poltergeist is actually someone in another realm, trying to get a response from you.

I'm not sure that's likely, but it's worth considering. It's also a good reason to treat a ghost as if it's a living person who might feel that you're an intruder in *their* home.

Generally, I don't recommend provoking except in extreme cases, and under the supervision of a respected professional prepared to deal with the after-effects.

32

EIFs and Other Geeky Topics

Want to travel down the rabbit hole? The following notes might be starting points for your research into more technical aspects of ghost hunting.

Experience Inducing Fields (EIFs)

Experience-inducing field, or EIF, is a term introduced by Dr. Jason Braithwaite, a cognitive psychologist and neuroscientist from the University of Birmingham.

Dr. Braithwaite did groundbreaking research at England's Muncaster Castle, the site of many reported hauntings.

The term "EIF" refers to any field responsible for inducing a particular experience. Dr. Braithwaite's early research suggested a connection between locations with magnetically remarkable signatures and repeated haunt-type experiences.

EIFs include sites with high levels of EMF. We know they can create emotional, mental, and physical distress.

Infrasound is an issue. I've often discussed the relationship between hauntings – particularly poltergeist activity – and underground streams, as well as water in general.

Most paranormal discussions practically ignore geomagnetic fields (GMFs). We need to include these in our surveys and consider them when evaluating others' reports and our own apparent experiences.

Early studies suggest that this kind of magnetic anomaly can affect 20 - 30% of people.

However, for years, I've been asking something radical: What if those fields also act as *beacons* for... well, whatever's reported at the location? (Some EM pump studies suggest I may been right about this, but it's far too early to know for certain.)

Whether or not the beacon concept has any merit, we need to examine EIFs more closely.

For example, they may explain some or all of the paranormal patterns – including "ley lines" – that I'm currently plotting and studying.

Before we assume that anything is actually a ghost, the subject of EIFs needs far greater exploration.

Recommended reading

Magnetic Hallucinations, by Maurice Townsend

http://www.assap.org/newsite/articles/Magnetic%20ghosts.html

For additional insights to ponder: Sleeping with the Entity, by Jason Braithwaite and Maurice Townsend.

http://bham.academia.edu/JasonJBraithwaite/Papers/242948/Sleeping_with_the_Entity

Fear cages

Elevated EMF (electromagnetic fields) in a confined area seems to produce anxiety and/or unusual reactions in some people.

Examples include a basement, closet, bathroom, or other small room with high EMF levels.

They're sometimes nicknamed "fear cages," a term popularized when Jason Hawes and Grant Wilson used it, particularly during the Season Four (2008) episode of Ghost Hunters, called "The Fear Cage."

To deal with a "fear cage," you'll probably need to address *both* issues (EMF and sense of confinement).

First, check for EMF levels, discussed near the beginning of this book.

After resolving EMF issues, you may need to relieve the sense of confinement or claustrophobia in that room.

Here are some suggestions:

- Remove shades, shutters, or dark curtains, or replace them with thin, light (not light-*blocking)* curtains.

- Some people prefer window blinds to shades.

- Paint the room a light color. Pale blue and light, neutral green (often used in hospitals for their calming effect) are the most popular choices.

- Add posters or art with pleasant scenery.

Those might help... or they might not. You won't know until you try it.

Learning from "Philip"

I believe "hauntings" may be caused by various circumstances, influences, and entities.

The 1976 book, *Conjuring Up Philip*, documented a significant study. It's a remarkable work based on a Canadian project by the Toronto Society of Psychical Research. (That book is currently out of print and difficult to find.)

The group deliberately created a possible (but fictional and deliberately error-filled) biography for Philip, an imaginary aristocratic Englishman from the 17th century.

Then, the group attempted to cause Philip to manifest as a ghost.

For months, nothing happened. Then, "Philip" began to knock on a table, once for yes or twice for no.

Significant physical evidence followed, and it was documented in the 1974 film Philip: The Imaginary Ghost.

In addition, during a visit to Canada, I interviewed one of the participants. He seemed wholly credible.

The ghostly manifestations were among the most intense ever recorded and thoroughly documented.

That astonishing magnitude of phenomena resulted from deliberate, objective research efforts by people who *knew* there was no Philip.

My question is: What could happen when people firmly *believe* in a particular ghost?

I don't have a reasonable explanation for this.

All possibilities must be considered when we're looking for the cause of a haunting and how to relieve it.

33

Safety Tips

Even in the most haunted settings, the world of the living can be more dangerous than anything ghostly. The causes are usually so mundane, we don't think about them until it's too late.

A typical home investigation can turn deadly... even when it's your own home.

In 2012, a young, otherwise healthy paranormal investigator died from a life-threatening respiratory complaint. It was the result of conducting research at a site with rodent droppings. Her team had visited that site, as had countless others.

The problem isn't just bat, rat, and mouse excrement. Consider the following safety issues and take precautions.

• Structural issues – Attic floorboards can be old and unable to support much weight. Ask the owner (or a home repair person or construction expert) before you venture up there.

• Dust in attics isn't just an issue when you're trying to take credible orb photos. It's also an allergen for many people.

• Basements are prone to mold and mildew. The problems may not be evident on cement or stone walls until someone starts wheezing.

• In cities and warm climates where cockroaches are a steady problem, it's not always the insects *but their droppings* that present the worst respiratory challenges.

• Histoplasmosis – Bat droppings can put you at risk in garages, attics, and basements. Histoplasmosis can be a severe respiratory disease and a significant threat in some areas. As it said on the website Bats and Rabies, "To be safe, avoid breathing dust in areas where there are animal droppings... wear a respirator that can guard against particles as small as two microns."

Since most of these issues are respiratory, every researcher should have – at the very least – a few simple medical masks in their ghost-hunting kit.

However, not all blue medical masks protect at the level you need. Read the label!

Essential facts about airborne risks and medical masks

• Airborne risks in dusty locations aren't news. Since speculation about "King Tut's Curse," people have been concerned about airborne diseases. That's especially true at locations where bodies may have been stored (including abandoned hospital morgues), murder sites, a cemetery's receiving vault, or tombs.

• The Center for Disease Control and Prevention (CDC) lists a wide range of rodent-related diseases, from Hanta to plague to one form of meningitis. Most are spread by "breathing in dust contaminated with rodent urine or droppings." Shortly before Sara Harris' 2012 death, I'd indicated a large mouse or rat in a ghost hunting video. Frankly, many of us in this field investigate sites where mice and rats had once been (or still are), and they've left droppings.

• Studies of SARS and other diseases have shown that dry particles can travel surprising distances and still cause infection.

• Traditionally, *surgical* masks are designed to protect the *environment* from the *wearer,* not vice versa. If you're buying blue masks, keep this in mind. Depending on their design, those blue masks usually test between 15% and 80% effective. The best are designed to filter the tiniest particles and have something at the nose so air isn't entering and exiting, unfiltered, at the top edge of the mask.

• Masks usually filter particles; they don't disinfect anything. If you have significant health issues leaving you incredibly vulnerable, or you're going to extremes, look for military-grade gas masks designed to protect from chemical and biological agents, as well as pandemics. (You may have seen investigators such as Zak Bagans wearing one on TV shows.) At that level, you'll achieve maximum protection.

• Masks do not filter out carbon monoxide or other toxic gases.

More precautions, beyond masks

Indoors (with no open windows), it may help to set up an air purifier ahead of time, if it's designed to HEPA standards. (HEPA filters remove more than 99% of airborne particles, usually down to 0.3 microns.)

However, most air purifiers are designed to filter tobacco smoke, pollen, and dust, not chemical or bacterial agents. Make sure the air purifier removes dust, and choose an air purifier with a CADR rating of at least 2/3 the square footage of the space you need to treat. (So, if it's a room with 120 square feet, you're looking for a CADR rating that's at least 80.)

Remember that your hands, hair, and clothing can pick up the same particles that you use a mask to avoid. So, keep your mask on when you shake your hair to dislodge particles and change your clothes. Disposable gloves – available in bulk from many pharmacies and beauty salon supply stores (like Sally Beauty Supply) – can be helpful when you might have to touch items that put you at risk, or in locations coated with dirt or dust.

I'm not trying to frighten you, especially if you're already worried about ghosts.

On the other hand, it's easy to be too casual about health and safety risks. A ten-cent medical mask can help protect your health, reduce your chances of an allergic reaction or asthma, and – in extreme cases – it might save your life.

Precautions will vary from person to person and from one investigation site to another. Someone investigating in northern Maine and eastern Canada will have very different concerns than someone investigating in Louisiana or an area affected by flooding. Someone with severe allergies or respiratory issues will take different precautions than someone who rarely catches a cold and enjoys exceptionally good immunity.

Before you do anything else...

Check carbon monoxide levels at the possibly haunted site.

Carbon monoxide is nicknamed "the silent killer." Pets and children often react to it first.

Carbon monoxide (CO), also called carbonous oxide, is a colorless, odorless, and tasteless gas.

In higher quantities, it is highly toxic to humans and animals. The gas can come from various sources, including gas appliances, wood stoves, car exhaust, blocked flues, and even cigarette smoke.

Some people are highly sensitive to carbon monoxide, and they may show symptoms before others do. Any of the following symptoms may indicate high levels of carbon monoxide.

• Headaches.
• A tight sensation in the chest.
• Nausea.
• Shortness of breath.
• Vomiting.
• Dizziness.
• Fatigue.
• A feeling of weakness.
• Confusion or disorientation.
• Visual disturbances.
• Fainting and seizures.
• Flu symptoms.
• Infants may be irritable.
• Pets can avoid certain areas.

To me, that sounds like a normal list of concerns from people who think they've encountered a ghost.

But wait, there's more: Carbon monoxide can also affect the heart and central nervous system, and raise blood pressure. Carbon monoxide poisoning can damage the fetus of a pregnant woman.

Many areas in the UK, America, and Canada have laws recommending (or even requiring) carbon monoxide detectors in homes. Older homeowners may not realize that.

Even if the homeowner has no fireplace, wood stove, or gas appliances, check the levels anyway.

For example, if a nearby neighbor has a wood stove and you (or the clients) sleep with a window open, elevated carbon monoxide could explain some "symptoms" of a haunting. Does a neighbor smoke outdoors or work on his car in the driveway? Could that air be pulled into the client's home through an air conditioner or window fan?

If you regularly investigate haunted sites, check carbon monoxide levels in *your own home*. If you've been sensitized, even low levels at a "haunted" site might trigger your symptoms, making you think the investigation site is haunted, too. Rule this out, immediately.

When *any* symptoms match the warning list, carbon monoxide levels must be checked first.

If the homeowner does not have a carbon monoxide detector installed, and you don't have a handheld or plug-in monitor, call the fire department for advice.

Also, though the *home* may not be the source of the carbon monoxide, something nearby might be. Heavy traffic is a common culprit. Apps are available that identify local, current (recent, or average) carbon monoxide levels by GPS, so you can also tell if that's a possible factor.

Air quality matters. It can be the invisible cause of discomfort at a possibly haunted site.

34

Haunted House Checklist

This list reminds you of the main things to check when investigating a possibly haunted home or business. This book includes other things you can look for, but if you have just a few hours to evaluate the home, this list covers the key points.

____ Carbon monoxide levels okay?

____ Obvious health or safety issues?

___Residents keep a diary of ghostly phenomena.

___Look for triggers at the site: Ouija boards, unusual religious displays, haunted objects

___EMF check - baseline, elevated EMF, or anomalous spikes.

___Floors level?

___Stairs level? Even and consistent heights? Stair rails, too?

___Windows & doors correctly hung? Latches secure?

___Signs of mold or mildew? Household allergies?

___Evidence of animals in walls, ceilings, attic, basement, crawl-space?

___Plumbing, heating, and a/c noises.

___Drafts (candle check).

___Hot spots, cold spots (hand and thermometer checks).

___Vibrations (traffic, trains, air traffic, nearby music, or other).

___Underground streams/springs (geological maps).

___Magnetic fluctuations around the site (survey property).

___Reactions of pets? (note where, when).

___Poltergeist possibilities? Spiritual concerns?

___Anything else? (Ask the homeowner or tenant, and check with neighbors.)

35

Ghost Questions, Answered

These are a few of my answers from "101 Ghost Hunting Questions, Answered." I'm including them here because they may explain more about ghosts and haunted places. Some were lightly edited for this book.

<u>What is a ghost?</u>

When people use the word "ghost," they usually mean something that seems ghostly, like an apparition, or an object that appears to move all by itself.

They may mean something as simple as a "creepy feeling," or something as frightening as a ghostly voice, or a chilling touch by an invisible hand.

Dictionaries say a ghost is the spirit of a dead person.

That may be true.

Or... that might be groundless, popular opinion. No two ghost hunters are likely to agree.

When paranormal investigators use the word "ghosts," we usually refer to ghostly phenomena, such as objects moving by themselves, and strange noises, including whispers, voices, and even music.

Opinions differ.

Some ghost hunters insist that all ghostly phenomena are signs of disembodied spirits.

Skeptics prefer rational explanations for "hauntings" and do not think they're supernatural.

A few religions insist that everything ghostly is demonic and dangerous.

Most ghost hunters are between those extremes. We say that ghostly phenomena are natural but unexplained.

First, we look for everyday things that might explain what's going on.

About 80% of the time, we can find a reasonable, normal explanation. The other 20% may be ghostly.

This is important: Even though some – or most – "ghostly" phenomena can be blamed on something normal, the site may still be haunted.

To draw a sports parallel: During a football game, most people on the field are football players. That doesn't mean the occasional streaker or the team mascot is also a football player. One could logically ask, "How did that streaker get past security?" or, "What is that mascot doing on the field when the teams are still mid-quarter?"

Logic doesn't matter. The streaker or mascot is there.

So, maybe most ghostly phenomena at a location can be explained. That doesn't mean it's not caused by a ghost.

Also, few investigators agree on all paranormal issues.

For every person who insists that all orbs are ghosts, you'll find one who says all orbs are dust or insects.

The truth may be somewhere in between.

In fact, I believe that the "ghosts" label is too simplistic.

Yes, most will agree that a ghost usually represents a deceased person. And maybe that's true.

What's still unknown is how much ghostly phenomena are actually caused by ghosts... and exactly what each one is.

Is a ghost alive or dead?

It depends upon the ghost, and it depends on how you define "alive."

I believe that the spirit of the person remains alive. (In this plane of existence, that person's body is lifeless. That's a semantic issue.)

In general, I believe that ghosts are as alive as you and I are. Despite that, we usually refer to ghosts as "spirits of the dead."

One ghostly exception: Some hauntings don't seem to be actual ghosts. They're more like energy imprints – often called "residual energy hauntings" – that linger at a location after something dramatic happens.

It's like walking into a room where two people have recently argued. Sometimes, you can still feel the crackle of hostile energy in the room.

Some people (and at least a few ghosts) object to the "living v. dead" distinction.

When that's an issue, I rely upon words like ghost, spirit, and entity. Some are okay with the word "deceased."

Also, when possible, I always refer to each ghost by their assumed name. That seems to help us get a response.

For example, although we're not sure the most famous ghost at the Myrtles Plantation was actually called "Chloe," we use that name for her anyway.

When I'm ghost hunting at the Myrtles, and I want to speak with that ghost, I'll say, "Chloe, I'd like to talk with you," and then say whatever is on my mind.

Also, most ghosts seem to find very little humor related to death.

The jokes and puns at Disney's Haunted Mansion attraction may seem funny to you. (They strike me as funny, too.)

However, avoid morbid jokes during ghost investigations. (I'm talking about things like "dying to meet you," "feeling dead tired," and so on.)

Offending ghosts is a terrible idea if you want to learn more about them or gain their cooperation.

And, in some settings, joking about ghosts can be dangerous.

What's it like to live in a house that's haunted? Do people always have to leave their haunted houses if the ghosts won't leave?

Most haunted houses are relatively benign. I've lived in a few. Generally, it's like living with an invisible roommate. I don't mind that, as long as they're considerate.

However, some ghosts can be annoying. That's especially true if the ghost likes to turn lights on and off, adjust the volume on the TV, or turn a faucet on and leave the water running.

Downtown Houston's famous ghost

One of the most persistently annoying ghosts haunts downtown Houston, Texas. She is Mrs. Pamelia Mann, one of Houston's most famous madams.

Many evenings, the ghost of Mrs. Mann strolls around the Market Square block she once owned.

She visits ladies' rooms (toilets) in modern-day clubs and restaurants on that block.

Once she's in each ladies' room, she locks the door so others cannot enter. Then, she vanishes. The staff are not amused, because they have to keep unlocking the door at the request of impatient patrons.

However, the living and spirits of the dead usually find ways to stay out of each other's way.

Other famous haunted homes

At some locations, such as the Myrtles Plantation, the staff regard the ghosts as friends. Many people who live in haunted houses feel the same way about their ghosts.

I know one homeowner in Salem (MA, USA) who is highly protective of her ghost. Although the first floor of her haunted home is a shop, she won't allow anyone inside if she thinks they're looking for "her" ghost.

That's a little extreme.

The owners of the Lizzie Borden house seemed comfortable with that house's ghosts. (Personally, I was uneasy with whatever lingers in that house's basement.)

TV, movies, and reality

Many TV shows and movies present scary ghosts.

Reality is very different.

Once people become accustomed to their ghosts (and vice versa), some forget they live in a haunted house.

When I've lived in haunted houses, I've been unable to forget that the ghosts are there. Not for long, anyway.

Sometimes, I've been startled by an apparition floating across my kitchen.

Unearthly footsteps still surprise me when I'm tired, especially if the ghost has been silent for a while.

Despite that, living with ghosts can be easier than living with room-mates. Ghosts don't steal your food, come home drunk at night, or leave the toilet seat up.

I'm okay with that.

How can I see a ghost?

If you'd like to see a ghost, you may need to do a lot of ghost hunting.

Many long-time ghost hunters have never seen a ghostly figure. Not one that they were sure was there.

Apparitions - any ghost you can see with your eyes at the moment it appears - are rare.

Most of the time, people think they may have seen something, but - at the time - it surprised them so much, they didn't instantly think "ghost."

It may have been an unexplained flicker of light or a shadow. It might have been just part of a ghostly figure, like a face that was there one moment, and gone the next.

It could have been a full apparition they mistook for someone living, dressed in a costume. (That's common at some living history events.)

It may have been a full or partial apparition the person saw for just a second, out of the corner of their eye. And then, it was gone.

Appearances vary. Are they influenced by our expectations? We have no way to be certain.

A ghostly image might resemble a reflection in a window, mirror, or shiny surface like a tabletop.

It could be a shadowy figure, whether or not it's a "shadow person."

However, seeing something that looks "like a ghost" (solid or translucent) and realizing it's a ghost while you still see it... that's extraordinary.

In other words, be observant if you want to see a ghost. Look very closely at the things that make you do a quick double-take.

You won't be sure it was a ghost until minutes after it's vanished. And, even then, you may have doubts.

Keep your expectations low. Don't insist you must see a ghost to believe in them.

Some people see anomalies. Some only photograph them. Others hear strange sounds or voices. Yet others only record them. And so on.

As you investigate haunted sites, you'll develop a "sixth sense" related to your unique way of tuning in to ghosts.

If you're like many people, it may not be anything visual.

Few actually see a ghost, but - if you do - it can be a moment you'll never forget.

What happens if someone sees a ghost?

The simple answer is: Nothing happens to them.

They've seen something that looked like a ghost.

That's all.

I'm sorry if that's disappointing. It happens to be the truth.

After decades of paranormal research, I'm used to ghosts and things that look like ghosts.

Seeing an apparition – or any other evidence of ghosts – may change a person's reaction to ghost stories.

Aside from the emotional and cognitive impact, I don't think anything else happens to the person.

No one dies from it.

The person isn't cursed.

People who see ghosts aren't personally haunted for the rest of their lives.

If you see a ghost, that's usually described as an *apparition*. An apparition often looks like a person or at least part of one. You might see a torso or a face. The apparition might be solid, translucent (it lets light through), or nearly transparent.

Generally, the ghost appears as they want to be remembered.

Few apparitions look gory, gruesome, or even elderly. When someone thinks they've seen something creepy... it's rarely a ghost. (That's important.)

Seeing a ghost is like witnessing any other extraordinary (but natural) event. It's an unusual experience, like seeing the Aurora Borealis or visiting an active volcano.

Maybe it's memorable. Perhaps the viewer would prefer to explain it as "an overactive imagination" or "the power of suggestion."

I never try to convince someone they've seen a ghost, even if I'm 99% sure they did.

Spiritual context can make a difference

Seeing a ghost might be startling, mainly if the person had been a skeptic.

To a believer, it affirms the idea of an afterlife.

We can't prove anything, one way or the other. All we can say is that the person believes he (or she) saw something like a ghost.

That's a personal, subjective experience.

Seeing a ghost might answer some people's questions: Yes, ghosts are real. After that, the individual may quit ghost hunting.

Or, the experience might trigger new questions, and the researcher may be even more enthusiastic about ghost hunting.

Meanwhile, nothing terrible happens to a person who's seen a ghost. Real life is different from movies and TV shows.

And, to be honest, apparitions are extremely rare. Most ghost hunters never see a ghost... not one they're *sure* was a ghost, anyway.

You're more likely to win the lottery.

How can I pitch a location to a ghost hunting TV show?

Would you like *your* haunted house to be featured on TV?

It's best to wait until ghost hunting TV shows request locations and story suggestions.

You'll find those requests online.

Look for specific paranormal TV shows and the production companies that cast and film them.

Check casting calls listed at websites like http://www.realitywanted.com/

You may also find opportunities on the HARO lists. http://www.helpareporter.com/

Be prepared

For the best success, you should:

Know the history of the location.

Know if it's ever been featured on a TV show (of any kind) in the past.

Know who owns the site, and exactly how to contact them.

Take lots of photographs at the location in daylight and during the hours the show would probably be filming.

Have a list of witnesses to the ghostly phenomena. They must be willing to talk to TV producers about their experiences, even if they're not paid for their time.

Many production companies like to film several shows in the same vicinity. For best success, be ready to present three or four other haunted locations in the same town or nearby.

If you're just scouting locations, the producers might not involve you in the filming. This means no screen credit unless you negotiate for it.

My advice is to present the one story that most interests you. Then, mention that you have several nearby locations equally suited to the TV show.

Take precautions

Before you reveal those other locations:

Get a written agreement signed by someone authorized by the production company. (Double-check that with someone highly ranked at the company.)

Hire an entertainment lawyer to review the contract.

Be clear about your continued obligations to the show or producers. For example, they may expect you to appear at events. Know how much time they expect and who will pay for your expenses.

Make sure you'll receive the full benefit of – and credit for – all of your work and creativity.

Understand what you can (and can't) say during and after the show airs. Know how long your non-disclosure terms will extend after the final episode.

Some liabilities of ghost hunting TV shows

Learn from my mistakes.

Never expect TV producers – or people who claim to be producers – to be honest or even logical. Get everything in writing... printed and signed, not just emailed.

Know exactly what's expected and what you'll get in return.

I was on one TV series for a major cable network that's viewed internationally and focused on history. But, even to promote the show, my contract prohibited me from saying I'd appeared on it.

Yes, that seems very weird. The producers seemed to think it was a standard requirement.

Then there's the time that, with a verbal agreement and lots of phone calls and emails confirming it, I spent three weeks scouting locations for a TV series.

That involved lots of driving, hours in dusty libraries and creepy locations, and conversations with a few truly strange people who wanted to tell me their ghost stories.

Was it fun...? Yes, most of the time.

Would I do it again...? No. I would not work 12+ hours a day, seven days a week, under a lot of pressure from the producer.

After that, I compiled the information the producer needed, including photos, ghost stories, verified site contacts, and witnesses, and sent it to them.

And then... The production company said their producer "hadn't been authorized" to hire me. Even with the star of the show and my manager working on this, I was never paid a cent. Sadly, my story is far from unique. It's just so embarrassing, others in the field rarely talk about similar experiences.

Don't let your eagerness cloud your judgment when dealing with producers. Before committing to anything, consult a theatrical agent, attorney, or both. Of course, if you're happy to work for nothing, just to know you were part of a TV show, go for it.

However, no matter what is implied, make sure you have it in writing, in actual ink on actual paper that you have in your hand. Be sure it's signed by someone with the authority to make that agreement.

What's the difference between a haunted object and a haunted house?

Frankly, it can be difficult to tell the difference. Mostly, it's a case of trial-and-error. *The Haunted Collector* TV series presented a basic view of what's involved.

From my experience, the size of the haunting could be a hint. Characteristics can vary, too.

Most actively haunted houses have distinct, ghostly phenomena. The ghost may appear in just one room or a variety of locations throughout the home. You sense that a spirit is involved. It's aware of you. It responds to what you do, and it's not the same activity, over and over again.

Other haunted houses might have residual energy. For example, a cold spot may appear at about 10 PM every night. It's likely to last around 20 minutes. If nothing else happens, it's probably just ghostly energy stored at the site.

Space clearing can reduce or eliminate that kind of problem.

But. a haunted object can affect an entire house, too.

A haunted or cursed object can affect a small area, a room, an entire floor, or the whole house.

It's smart to investigate using an EMF meter. See if one object is the focal point of the ghostly activity. Unless an object is magnetized or runs on electricity, it shouldn't affect your EMF meter.

If you suspect an object is haunted

Here's the simplest way to see if an object might be haunted, and if it's the source of the ghostly activity at the site.

1. Remove the object.
2. Take it several miles away.
3. See if the issues stop.

If everything seems normal (or gradually becomes normal after a week or two), the problem was probably the object. Don't burn it. Contact someone like John Zaffis. He's an expert in that field. (He's also very different from how he's seemed on TV.)

Unfortunately, tests like this require a lot of trial and error. The process can be nightmarish if the house contains more than one haunted object.

In the 19th century and early 20th century, newspapers often discussed haunted and cursed objects. For example, many people still recall tales of the curse of the Hope Diamond.

However, that may be the only haunted object they recall. Until the Haunted Collector TV series highlighted haunted objects, they'd been pretty much forgotten.

As a result, few ghost hunters know how to find haunted objects, and even fewer are experts in the field.

I have no idea what percentage of haunted houses are actually plagued by haunted objects. At this point in our research, it's impossible to guess.

Energy from a ghost and energy from a haunted object... well, they're different. It's difficult to articulate.

How to detect a haunted object

Old, everyday objects can be haunted. They don't have to "look creepy."

First, when I'm near a haunted or cursed object, my reaction is more like, "Uh-oh. Something is not right, here."

In my head, I can practically hear the shark-is-on-the-way music from the movie, "Jaws." I'm uneasy. I feel unsafe.

Investigating, I usually zero-in on an object. That's when I'll tell the owner to remove whatever-it-is before I return for a more complete investigation.

Haunted houses...? No problem.

For me, haunted objects are a different matter.

I absolutely, positively do not like haunted objects. And, among haunted objects, creepy dolls are the very worst... in my opinion, anyway. Some defaced photos and advertising images are a close second.

Note: If you have a haunted object, there's a steady interest in them at auction sites like eBay.

How do people talk to ghosts?

We're asking ghosts to talk to us. But are we certain the spirits hear *us* when we talk to ghosts?

I'm not sure many ghost hunters have considered this issue.

Sure, look at past episodes of ghost-hunting TV shows like Ghost Hunters or Ghost Adventures. You'll see "ghosts" talking to investigators through ghost hunting tools, from loosened flashlights to EVP recordings to real-time communications devices.

However, that may not be your question.

You're likely asking how ghosts communicate with us.

Researchers like me don't use Ouija boards to talk to ghosts. We speak out loud to them.

That should be a clear distinction. Could a board help ghosts hear you? It's possible, but I'm not sure that it's likely. (Also, I consider Ouija boards, spirit boards, etc., dangerous in the hands of those who don't understand the risks. John Zaffis and others have explained this on YouTube and other sites. (Their concerns are legitimate.)

I'm not sure that ghosts have difficulty receiving messages from us.

Talk as if they're alive and in human form

In many cases, when someone is troubled by a ghost in their home, my advice is, "Just talk to your ghosts, out loud."

So far, readers have reported success with this.

However, they may have a special connection with their ghosts. After all, they share the same space, day in and day out. That may improve communication across the divide.

I've had mixed results when I've talked out loud to ghosts at haunted sites I've visited.

For example, at Gilson Road Cemetery (Nashua, NH), I sense that the ghosts don't care if I talk to them.

Oh, they've misbehaved when I've investigated that site with skeptics. (That always amuses me, but that's my sense of humor.)

They also manifest in various ways when researchers are there. But do ghosts care what we say to them? I have no idea.

Is talking even necessary?

We may not need to talk to ghosts in places such as England's Stratford-upon-Avon. Some of those spirit entities seem to read our minds.

For example, at Falstaff's Experience/Tudor World (Stratford-upon-Avon, England), at least one ghost responded to almost everything that was said.

He also seemed to read thoughts. It was disconcerting.

Between the extremes of Gilson Road Cemetery and Tudor World, ghosts have responded inconsistently, even at very active sites.

Other options

Maybe we need to try other means. Many of us - including me - have assumed that some ghosts are hanging on every word we utter.

But what if they hear only 10% of what we say, or less?

There's a lot to consider.

For example, maybe ghosts can read what we write. After all, some investigators practice variations of "automatic writing," and those words seem to communicate to – and come from - somewhere.

Get creative!

Of course, there are additional ways ghosts can reply to us. Pendulums work for some. Others like dowsing rods, and assign one kind of movement to "yes" and another to "no." And so on. (Note: All have the same spiritual risks as Ouija boards, and should not be used casually.)

Perhaps we need to try new, fresh approaches.

Can spirits detect EMF spikes on their side of the veil? Perhaps we could try repeatedly turning EMF-generating appliances (or tools) on and off to get the ghosts' attention.

Maybe they can sense us better when we're near a mirror or a doll, especially one that's supposed to be haunted.

Since some ghosts seem to interact with flashlights, perhaps they sense other light sources, too. Maybe you can get their attention by turning a bright light on and off several times.

Possibly, they can hear music. You could try whistling or singing.

Or... Well, this could be a very long list.

These are just a few suggestions. You may think of others.

For now, simply talking out loud seems to be the most reliable.

And, in general, I think it's time to explore better ways to communicate with ghosts, instead of focusing exclusively on better ways to hear from them.

Is there any scientific proof of ghosts?

For skeptics who ask that in a snarky tone and with a raised eyebrow, I reply in kind: There is no scientific "proof" of ghosts or anything else in paranormal research... or many other types of research.

"Proofs" come from mathematics and logic.

Science relies on *evidence,* and much of it is provisional.

Scientists constantly improve their techniques and research methods. Thanks to a steady supply of new discoveries, there is no final word in science, which makes it an exciting, evolving field.

So, while this may seem like a finicky, semantic point, there is no proof.

If you want conclusive, scientific evidence of ghosts, it doesn't exist yet.

You may find an answer that makes sense to you. It might be all the evidence you need.

Scientific evidence is something else.

We can go to a haunted site and – often but not always – trigger unexplained phenomena. However, our results aren't consistent.

In other words, ghostly phenomena can't be duplicated to lab standards. Never mind "scientific proof of ghosts." We don't even have reliable scientific evidence at this point.

If we could reliably duplicate what we encounter at haunted sites, we might find better answers to many ghost hunting questions.

People have tried to understand ghosts for centuries, but we're still far from turning this into a credible science.

For now, there's no "proof." We can't convince skeptical critics that ghosts are real, either.

Of course, there may never be enough evidence for that.

Many people believe what they want to believe, period. After all, some people still insist the world is flat, and nothing will persuade them otherwise.

I'd love to claim that there is scientific proof of ghosts, but there isn't and – in my opinion – perhaps never will be.

What we're actually searching for is scientific evidence of ghosts.

In that context, we're making good progress.

What's the connection between ghosts and demons?

Ghosts and demons may be connected.

Or... they may not be.

Let's say that ghosts are the spirits of people who once lived among us.

By contrast, I think that most will agree that – at least in most spiritual contexts – demons never lived as humans.

They are very different kinds of beings.

Some religions don't believe in Satan, the Devil, or similar entities.

Usually, those religions don't believe any entity could significantly threaten Deity. In fact, among those particular religions, it's heresy to believe in a mighty, Devil-like being.

However, if spirits exist, some seem to have better intentions than others.

At extremes, some spirits may be benevolent and described in angelic terms. Others seem to thrive on evil and malicious behavior.

Many investigators use the word "demon" to describe energy representing something profoundly malicious. It's a relative term with many variations.

Ghosts aren't always well-behaved. Some may be pranksters or naughty, like poltergeists. Others can be angry or territorial. They may influence or invade our physical world, touching or hitting and scratching investigators.

Those ghosts can be frightening.

Nevertheless, there is a distinction between ghosts and demons.

Demons' intentions seem dangerously different. Most first-person encounters suggest that demonic energy is intent on fooling us, so we drop our defenses.

Then, it attacks.

Crossovers may exist. Some ghosts were, and perhaps still are, under the influence of demons.

If a spirit seems malicious, I avoid it.

If danger is possible at any site, I leave it. You should, too.

I'd rather be too cautious than spend months - or even years - regretting a foolhardy moment.

I've listened to demonologists I trust, like John Zaffis and the late Father Andrew Calder. Their tales have been terrifying and convincing.

However, evidence suggests that ghosts do not become demons, and demons do not become ghosts.

So, there seems to be no direct connection between them.

Ghosts and demons are different kinds of entities in the spirit world. When they interact with us, their behaviors are very different.

Ghost hunters can encounter both of these entities at a single site. There may be other entities we haven't fully identified yet. (I'm thinking about cryptids and faeries, etc.)

Focus on ghosts. If anything else seems to intrude, it's best to leave if you feel threatened.

What's your theory about ghosts and alternate dimensions?

This may seem radical, but I believe that some "ghosts" are people who are alive and well in a parallel world.

Perhaps the veil (or membrane) between us is thinner at some geographical locations. Related legends date back to the earliest recorded history.

Nevertheless, I'm certain many hauntings have nothing to do with "dead people."

We've seen glimmers of this possibility throughout history. Stories of doppelgängers could be explained in quantum terms.

Some paranormal researchers believe that EVP could be a recent energy echo even within our world and time.

For example, archaeologist and ghost excavator John Sabol recorded an EVP that sounded *exactly* like a previous investigation by Jason Hawes and Grant Wilson at the same location.

Was that a time echo? We don't know.

Some spirits may be visiting us from the other side. If they are, I think they represent a small percentage of the entities and phenomena we label "ghostly."

I'm closely watching studies related to gravity. It's an anomaly. Gravity doesn't make sense.

As explained in the Wikipedia entry about five-dimensional space, "Physicists have speculated that the graviton, a particle thought to carry the force of gravity, may 'leak' into the fifth or higher dimensions, which would explain how gravity is significantly weaker than the other three fundamental forces."

So, EMF may also be leaking into our universe.

Better answers may emerge as we understand more about discrepancies and flows connected with gravity and higher dimensions. They may help us understand parallel realities, the beings that inhabit them, and those that seem to interact with us.

Yes, that may sound completely "sci-fi," but consider this: If you try to explain electric lights to some ghosts, they react with equal skepticism... and often think we're demons.

For now, I'm keeping an open mind.

I like the idea of alternate dimensions and realities. I think they're among the best explanations for some (not all) odd things we encounter in ghost hunting.

Do I take any of this *seriously...?* Of course not. I have fun speculating and building fantastical theories by placing one "what if...?" upon another. That's all.

—

If you liked these questions and answers...

Read my book, "101 Ghost Hunting Questions, Answered." It's available at Amazon and other book sellers, and your public library may have a copy or be able to get one through inter-library loan.

36

About the Author

Fiona Fitzgerald Broome is an author, researcher, and paranormal analyst. Her ghost reports and stories have appeared in magazines such as *Fate* since the early 1980s.

Ms. Broome may be best known as the founder of HollowHill.com, one of the Internet's oldest, most extensive, and most respected paranormal websites.

Fiona flippantly describes herself as a "blip analyst." Her specialty is identifying the history and patterns that result in paranormal events and – perhaps – predicting where they'll happen next.

Fiona has written over 1000 ghost-related articles. She's also written more than 20 books and contributed to many others. They include *The Ghosts of Austin (Texas)*, *Ghost Hunting in Haunted Cemeteries*, *101 Ghost Hunting Questions - Answered*, *Weird Hauntings*, *Weird Encounters*, *Armchair Reader: Weird, Scary & Unusual*, and *Kick'n Back in Texas*.

She's working on a series of books documenting ghost stories and about the predictive side of paranormal research.

Fiona was raised near Boston, Massachusetts, and studied at Harvard and M.I.T. She's also a certified archaeological illustrator (Boston University) and a professional genealogist.

Fiona has worked as a consultant and location scout for various TV shows related to history, science, and paranormal encounters.

She welcomes visitors to her website, FionaBroome.com, where she writes about her current projects and plans.